Chance Encounters
TRAVEL TALES FROM
AROUND THE WORLD

ID701370

Edited by Janna Graber

WORLD TRAVELER PRESS
COLORADO, USA

story – the story of redemption.

The shedding of the innocent blood of an animal to provide a covering for Adam pointed all the way down through 4,000 years of time, to the afternoon when Jesus hung upon the cross of Calvary, and the Roman soldier pierced His side with a spear, pouring out that innocent blood upon the ground.

Throughout the Hebrew scriptures the word "blood" has a number equivalent of 148.

The number 148 is woven through the Bible's story of redemption because the redemption of man could only be accomplished through the shedding of blood – innocent blood. The writer of Hebrews stated it succinctly when he said, *"Without the shedding of blood there is no remission,"* (Heb. 9:22)

The number 148 is intricately woven through the Bible's story of redemption.

Soon after Adam left the Garden of Eden children were born to him. One of his sons, Abel, a keeper of flocks, offered an acceptable sacrifice to God. It was the offering of a lamb. The shedding of the innocent blood (148) of the lamb was the evidence of the scarlet thread of redemption.

Coming down through time approximately 2,000 years we find Abraham on Mount Moriah, building an altar and laying the wood in place for a fire. He had been instructed by God to offer his son, Isaac, as a sacrifice. It was more than anyone had ever asked of a father. As Isaac lay upon the altar, he was as good as dead, when suddenly the voice of an angel, sent from God, said comfortingly, *""Lay not thine hand upon the lad, neither do thou anything unto him: for now I know that thou fearest God, seeing thou hast not withheld thy son, thine only son from me."* (Gen. 22:12)

It was then that Abraham saw a ram, entangled by its horns in a thicket of briars. He took the ram and slew it, shedding its innocent blood (148), and placed it on the altar of sacrifice, instead of Isaac.

It is a touching story, and I seldom can read it without finding tears running down my face. It was the enactment of a real live drama that pictures an event that would take place 2,000 years into the future – the event of God offering His only Son on Calvary's cross. The innocent blood of the ram, in the place of Isaac, pictured the innocent blood of Jesus Christ that poured from His side and ran down His precious body, dripping onto the ground below.

A few years after Abraham had returned home with Isaac, he sent his servant to find his son a bride. She was young and barren, but after twenty years, she finally bore to Isaac twin sons – Jacob and Esau.

Jacob, whose name was changed to Israel, had twelve sons, who became the fathers of the twelve tribes of Israel. At the age of 147, Jacob knew that he was near death, so he called his twelve sons to gather around his bed. As was the custom, he gave a short prophecy regarding the future of each son.

To his son, Judah, he said: *"The sceptre shall not depart from Judah, nor a lawgiver from between his feet until Shiloh come; and unto him shall the gathering of the people be."* (Gen. 49:10) Judah was promised the "sceptre." It was actually a prophecy indicating that Judah would be a ruler. And, indeed, Judah's descendants became kings, beginning with King David and continuing through all the kings of the nation of Judah. Jesus Christ was born of this line from Judah, and it is prophesied of Him that He will be a King on David's throne forever.

Judah also had twin sons. But when Tamar, who bore them to Judah, was in labor, a strange thing happened. One of the twins put forth his hand. The midwife, thinking that this child would be the firstborn, tied a scarlet thread around his wrist. However, this twin withdrew the hand, and the other twin came out first.

"And it came to pass, when she travailed, that the one put out his hand: and the midwife took and bound upon his hand a scarlet thread, saying, This came out first. And it came to pass, as he drew back his hand, that, behold, his brother came out: and she said, How hast thou broken forth? this breach be upon thee: therefore his name was called Pharez. And afterward came out his brother, that had the scarlet thread upon his hand: and his name was called Zerah." (Gen. 38:28-30)

I was curious about this text, and wondered if the scarlet thread would perhaps add to 148. It did not. However, upon further examination of the Hebrew text, I was thrilled to find that this event does indeed bear the number 1480. (In Gematria zeros are merely place holders and do not change the basic number.)

Reading the text as it appears in Hebrew, it says, *"tied on his hand scarlet."*

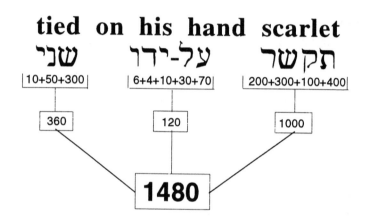

The Gematria of this text is absolutely marvelous! It produces not only 1480 but also the numbers 360, 120 and 1000. In this chapter I'm dealing only with the number 148, however, keep the other three numbers in mind. In succeeding chapters the numbers 360, 120 and 1000 will play a prominent role, for they are basic to the number patterns in the Gematria of the Bible.

It is good, here, to remind the reader that Hebrew reads from right to left. To make it easier to read the English, I have written the English words as they normally read from left to right, thus the numbers that appear under the words are the numbers for the Hebrew. In the above text the numbers are:

Tied	**1000**
On his hand	**120**
Scarlet	**360**

The Gematria for this simple short item of scripture is an outstanding display of the number code of the Bible. The numbers it produces are basic to the number patterns of the Bible, and the plain text is basic to the whole message that the Bible contains – the message of the scarlet thread of redemption. The redemption number is 148. This number repeats itself through the whole story of the redemption of man by the blood of Jesus Christ.

The story of redemption is told by the number 148.

Moving forward through the Genesis record of man's history, we read the story of the enforced slavery of the Israelites by the Egyptians. It was a time of great building for the nation of Egypt, but a time of suffering and bondage for the Israelites, and they pleaded to God for their deliverance. God heard their cries, and sent Moses to deliver them from the hand of Pharaoh.

When Moses asked leave from the Pharaoh, the answer was "No." But God made Pharaoh a little more willing by sending a series of plagues on the land of Egypt. After nine severe disasters upon the land, the final plague was the death of all the firstborn, both of humans and of the cattle. Even the firstborn son of the Pharaoh would die that night. But God had a plan whereby He would save the Israelites.

God instructed Moses to have each household of the Israelites kill a lamb, and sprinkle its blood around the door frames of their houses, so that when the death angel passed by, he would see the blood and save the firstborn of that household alive. Thus it became known as the Passover. That word, and that event, in the story of the scarlet thread of redemption is marvelous!

The killing of the lamb is a picture of the killing of Jesus; and the saving power of the blood of that lamb pictures the saving power of the blood of Jesus. The Apostle Paul made this unmistakably clear when he said, *"Christ, our Passover, is sacrificed for us,"* (I Cor. 5:7) It is no coincidence, and no mere fluke of history, that precisely 1,480 years (by Hebrew inclusive time) after Moses and the Israelites killed their Passover lambs that fearful night, that Jesus, the antitypical Passover Lamb, hung dying on the cross of Calvary. He was not only the great Passover Lamb, but He fulfilled the number code which pointed to this event. Jesus died on the afternoon when Israel's priests were killing the Passover lambs in commemoration of the night they left Egypt. God's timing is precise!

There were 1,480 years from the first Passover to the death of Jesus.

It was no coincidence that the word "Passover," in Hebrew, adds to 148; and the name "Christ," in Greek, adds to 1480. He was, indeed, the fulfilling of the prophecy, the type and the number code.

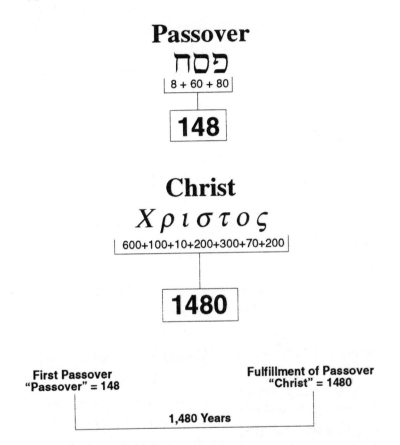

Passover

פסח

| 8 + 60 + 80 |

148

Christ

$X \rho \iota \sigma \tau o \varsigma$

| 600+100+10+200+300+70+200 |

1480

First Passover
"Passover" = 148

Fulfillment of Passover
"Christ" = 1480

1,480 Years

Let's return, briefly, to the time when Moses led the Israelites into the wilderness to escape from the hand of Pharaoh.

The desert wilderness was a dry and desolate place, and the people soon realized that they had no water. But God had already prepared for this event. He told Moses to strike a rock and water would come out. Now we all know that water does not flow from dry rocks. And the people probably wondered why Moses was doing such a foolish and fruitless thing. But they were astonished when an abundant stream of water came gushing out of the rock – enough water to quench the thirst of more than two million people plus their cattle and livestock. The water from the rock literally saved their lives.

Again, the Apostle Paul told us what it symbolized. He said *"And they all did drink the same spiritual drink; for they drank of that spiritual Rock that followed them: and that Rock was Christ,"* (I Cor. 10:4). The life-giving waters that flowed from the rock pictured the waters of life that Jesus provided for us when He died upon Calvary's cross. And just as the rock had to be smitten before the waters could gush out, so also Christ had to suffer and die in order to provide life for His human family.

This story of the water from the rock was never forgotten in Israel. It was incorporated into their songs of praise to God. In Psalm 105:41 we find the remembrance of it in praise:

1480 – He opened the rock and the waters gushed out; they ran in the dry places

"He opened the rock and the waters gushed out; they ran in the dry places." How amazing it is to realize that the total number values of every Hebrew letter in this statement add to 1480. Yes, the smiting of the rock and the gushing forth of the waters was part of the scarlet thread of redemption, and it bore the number 1480.

Moses was a faithful leader of the Israelites through

the forty years of their wilderness journey. He knew that he was a forerunner of their true deliverer who would be sent to them at some future time, for he said, *"The Lord thy God will raise up unto thee a Prophet from the midst of thee, of thy brethren, like unto me; unto him ye shall hearken,"* (Deut. 18:15). That true deliverer was Jesus Christ.

Thus, when it came time for Moses to die, God took him up into a mountain called Pisgah from which he could look out over the whole land that had been promised to them for an inheritance. But he was not allowed to enter it. God buried him there, probably at the foot of Pisgah near the east bank of the Jordan. The place of his death bore the number of the scarlet thread of redemption. Pisgah has a number value of 148.

Pisgah

פ ס ג ה

| 5 + 3 + 60 + 80 |

148

Moses knew that he was going to die on Mt. Pisgah, so before he climbed the mountain he appointed Joshua to be his successor as leader of the Israelites. It was Joshua who led them across the Jordan river and into the promised land. The name Joshua, in Hebrew, is the same as the name Jesus in Greek. Both mean "Saviour."

Before crossing over the Jordan, Joshua sent two men over to spy out the town of Jericho. The men went to the home of a woman named Rahab. She was a harlot, who lived in the wall of Jericho. She hid them briefly, then helped them escape by letting them down on the outside of the wall by a long cord that she tied from her window. Because she had helped them and had not reported them to the men of Jericho, the two spies gave her a solemn promise. She and her entire household would be saved when the army of the Israelites came into Jericho, but only if she would tie this same cord into her window. It was to be a signal to the Israelites that she was to be saved.

That cord is called, in the Hebrew scriptures, a scarlet thread. It was the means by which Rahab and her household would be saved from death. It pictures the means by which the entire family of Adam will be saved from death – by the blood of Jesus Christ. In the Hebrew text, this scarlet thread has a number value of 388. It is a number that is used in the Gematria of the Bible relating to the second coming of Jesus, and the time when He takes His rightful place on the throne of David.

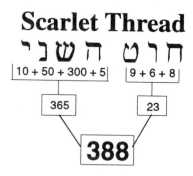

Scarlet Thread

The scarlet thread of redemption – the blood of Jesus – saves the family of Adam. And it was the scarlet thread that Rahab tied to her window that saved her family. The scarlet thread bore the number 388. It is a number associated with the coming of Jesus to take His rightful place on the throne of David. (Luke 1:32)

The throne of His father, David
τον θρονον Δαυιδ του πατρος αυτου

300+70+50+9+100+70+50+70+50+4+1+400+10+4+300+70+400+
80+1+300+100+70+200+1+400+300+70+400

3880

Shiloh comes
כי-יבא שילה

5+30+10+300 | 1+2+10+10+20

345 | 43

388

The Apostle Paul told us that the coming of Jesus would be accompanied by the sound of a trumpet. It is not a coincidence that the sounding of a trumpet in Hebrew bears the number 388.

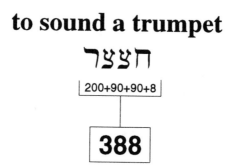

to sound a trumpet

חצצר

200+90+90+8

388

Yes, the Prophet whom God raised up, like unto Moses, was indeed Jesus Christ. His precious blood, shed on Calvary, was the fulfilling of all the types, pictures and events involving the scarlet thread. Solomon used the simile when describing the Beloved – *"Thy lips are like a thread of scarlet,"*(Song of Solomon 4:3). His lips speak the promise of life. He said, *"The words that I speak unto you, they are spirit and they are life,"* (John 6:63).

And just as Moses had provided a "way" in the desert for the Israelites, so Jesus proclaimed Himself to be the "Way" unto life. He told His disciples, *"I am the Way, the Truth, and the Life."* The "Way" of salvation is truly through Him. It is not surprising then to find that the "Way" bears the number 148.

Way

מ ע ג ל ה

| 5 + 30 + 3 + 70 + 40 |

148

We are told in scripture that *"The wages of sin is death,"* (Rom. 6:23). But Jesus did not die for any sin that He had committed. His death was a pure and undefiled offering as a substitute for Adam, who had forfeited his life through disobedience. The death of Jesus was the balancing of the scales of justice – a life for a life.

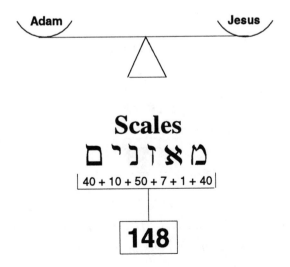

Scales

מ א ז נ י ם

| 40 + 10 + 50 + 7 + 1 + 40 |

148

The prophet Isaiah showed the exact balance – the exact price – that Jesus would pay for the sin of Adam. He

Jesus' innocent blood was the exact price for Adam's guilty blood.

said, *"Though your sins be as scarlet, they shall be as white as snow; though they be red like crimson, they shall be as wool,"* (Isaiah 1:18). Because of his disobedience, Adam's blood was required of him. But Jesus came as the Second Adam, providing the price – blood – that would redeem Adam.

Death had had victory over Adam. But because Jesus gave His life in place of the life of Adam, death no longer had the victory. The race of Adam had been redeemed – purchased by the pure and undefiled blood of Jesus. He was the first to receive victory over the grave. He was the "firstborn" from the dead. And through His victory He has provided a way that we might also have the victory.

Victory

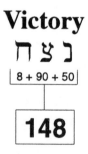

נ צ ח

| 8 + 90 + 50 |

148

The Apostle Paul said, *"Death is swallowed up in victory. O death, where is thy sting? O grave, where is thy victory?"* (I Cor. 15:54-55).

He was quoting from the prophecy of Isaiah: *"And he will destroy in this mountain the face of the covering cast over all people* (death)*, and the vail that is spread over all nations. He will swallow up death in victory; and the Lord God will wipe away tears from off all faces.... And it shall be said in that day, Lo, this is our God; we have waited for him, and he will save us: this is the Lord; we have waited for him, we will be glad and rejoice in his salvation."* (Isa. 25:7-9)

When Jesus was here on earth He continually talked about the Kingdom that He would establish. Most of His parables were about the promised Kingdom. His disciples did not understand that He talked of a future Kingdom. They were desirous of being released from their bondage to Rome, and hoped that He would establish His Kingdom at that time. But the

> **Jesus spoke often of the Kingdom that He would establish in the earth.**

Kingdom for which He taught them to pray was a future event. Had they known they would have to wait nearly 2,000 years they would probably have become discouraged. Even now, as we wait earnestly for His Kingdom to be established in the earth, we feel that the time is progressing too slowly. Oh how we long for that promised Kingdom!

It is encouraging to realize that the scarlet thread of redemption is still weaving its way through the history and future of man, and that the long-promised Kingdom is soon to be a reality. Yes, that Kingdom for which He taught us to pray also bears the number of the scarlet thread – 148.

His Kingdom

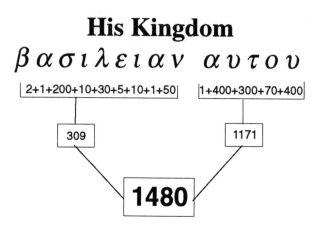

$$\beta \alpha \sigma \iota \lambda \epsilon \iota \alpha \nu \quad \alpha \upsilon \tau \upsilon$$

| 2+1+200+10+30+5+10+1+50 | 1+400+300+70+400 |

309   1171

1480

The prophet Isaiah foretold the birth of this future King, and of His Kingdom of justice and peace – a Kingdom that would never end.

"For unto us a child is born, unto us a son is given: and the government shall be upon his shoulder: and his name shall be called Wonderful, Counselor, The mighty God,

The Kingdom of peace that will never end.

The everlasting Father, The Prince of Peace. Of the increase of his government and peace there shall be no end, upon the throne of David, and upon his kingdom, to order it, and to establish it with judgment and with justice from henceforth even for ever," (Isaiah 9:6-7).

The scarlet thread of redemption has woven its way through 6,000 years of the history of man. The first part of Isaiah's prophecy has been fulfilled. The Child was born 2,000 years ago. Today we stand on the threshold of His promised Kingdom.

The tie that binds all history together into one grand and awesome plan is told in a simple number – 148. These three numerals are part of a vast and beautiful pattern – a pattern that tells the story of God's great plan for the salvation of man through the willing sacrifice of His Son, Jesus Christ.

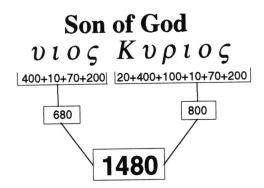

This book is a glimpse into those number patterns and the amazing relationship of the Word of God to the Works of God.

This is my ninth book on the subject of Gematria, and yet I have barely scratched the surface of a vast and awesome subject that appears to be as limitless as the wonders of God. Truly the patterns of Gematria that have been encoded into the Old and New Testaments further testify to the authenticity of the scriptures. The numbers show the same continuity throughout the entire Book that is told by the surface text. And although written over a period of approximately 2,000 years, it tells a consistent story – the story of the redemption of mankind by the blood of Jesus.

Summary of the scarlet thread of redemption and its Gematria.

148 = Blood

1480 = Tied on his hand scarlet

148 = Passover

1480 = Christ

1,480 years between the typical and antitypical Passover

1480 = He opened the rock and the waters gushed out; they ran in the dry places.

148 = Pisgah

148 = Way

148 = Scales (balances)

148 = Victory

1480 = His Kingdom

1480 = Son of God

388 = Scarlet thread

3880 = The throne of His father, David

388 = Shiloh comes

388 = To sound a trumpet

2
The Foundation

"Other foundation can no man lay than that is laid, which is Jesus Christ," (I Cor. 3:11).

We have seen the process by which the scarlet thread of redemption was illustrated through many stories and types, and was finally fulfilled by the shedding of the innocent blood of Jesus. The concept that His blood was shed for Adam (and consequently the race of Adam), is the very foundation of the whole plan of God for the salvation of man. Thus the Apostle Paul firmly stated *"Other foundation can no man lay."*

Secure foundations are essential for the constructing of any edifice. Let's look at the foundation – Jesus Christ. A study of this foundation, using the Gematria of the Bible, reveals some of the intricate beauty of the mind of God. We only get a glimpse, for it is not possible for us to see the whole. But some of these small glimpses are more than our human comprehension can grasp.

The ancient Hebrew scriptures reveal an intentional use of its Gematria to tell the same story that is told by its surface text. Some call it an ancient code. Others call it a God-code. Its authenticity has been proven by all those who have attempted its investigation. Even the traveling companion of the Apostle Paul, whose name was Barnabas, wrote concerning the interpretation of this ancient code. Quotations from his letter have been cited by Clemens Alexandrinus, Origen, Eusebius, and Jerome – the early fathers of Christianity. Barnabas gave us an insight into the use of Gematria in the Hebrew scriptures. He wrote:

> For the Scripture says that Abraham circumcised three hundred and eighteen men of his house. But what therefore was the mystery that was made known unto him? Mark first the eighteen, and next the three hundred. For the numeral letters of ten and eight are I H. And these denote Jesus. And because the cross was that by which we were to find grace; therefore he adds, three hundred: the note of which is T (the figure of his cross). Wherefore by two letters he signified Jesus, and by the third his cross.

In the ancient Hebrew scriptures we find the word "foundation" many times. Hebrew words often have different spellings for different meanings. Let's look at two of the occurrences of the word "foundation."

Foundation

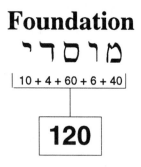

מוסדי

$$10 + 4 + 60 + 6 + 40$$

120

Foundation

יסד

| 4 + 60 + 10 |

74

These two numbers, 12 and 74, bear witness to the statement of the Apostle Paul that Jesus Christ is the one and only Foundation. Observe what happens when we multiply these two foundation numbers:

$$12 \times 74 = 888$$

Throughout the Greek scriptures (the New Testament) the name of Jesus bears the number 888. He is the multiplication of the two foundation numbers.

Jesus

Ιησους

| 10+8+200+70+400+200 |

888

The Apostle John told us that Jesus was the foundation of creation. He said, *"All things were made by him,*

and without him was not anything made that was made,"
(John 1:2). It is not surprising, then, to find that the word
"creation" also bears the foundation number, 74.

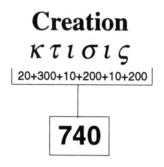

Creation

κ τ ι σ ι ς

| 20+300+10+200+10+200 |

740

The name Jesus is the multiplication of the foundation numbers 12 and 74. However, when we add 12 and 74 we get a total of 86. It is the Gematria for the *Elohim*, which is a plural word in Hebrew – the word used in Genesis 1:1: *"In the beginning God* (Elohim) *created the heaven and the earth."*

12 + 74 = 86

Elohim

אלהים

| 40+10+5+30+1 |

86

When we analyze these two foundation numbers, 12 and 74, we find them quite remarkable in their relation to the foundation principles of mathematics. The number 12 can be reduced to 3, its lowest prime factor. The number 74 can be reduced to 37, its highest prime factor. These two prime numbers, 3 and 7 are intricately interwoven into the very foundation of creation. For those who do not like math, bear with me for a moment. The following demonstration is not just a mathematical game. It is a basic principle of the creation of all things.

The number 37 is the twelfth prime. A prime number is one that is evenly divisible by no other number except 1. The first twelve primes are 2, 3, 5, 7, 11, 13, 17, 19, 23, 29, 31, and 37.

One of the principles of the number code of the Bible is that numbers can be read either left to right, or right to left. Thus the number 37 can also be read as 73. And likewise the number 12 can also be read as 21. This is because we are dealing with numerals and not quantity.

The 12th prime is 37. Reverse the numerals and the 21st prime is 73.

Thus we find that 37 is the 12th prime and 73 is the 21st prime. We have not only reversed the 37 and obtained 73, we have reversed the 12 and obtained 21. It appears to be a basic principle of creation.

The first verse of the Bible reads: *"In the beginning God created the heaven and the earth."* Adding all its number values we get a total of 2701. This is 37 x 73. The two basic numerals of the 12th prime and the 21st prime

– 3 and 7 – describe the creation of the heavens and the earth. It is magnificent!

By the same concept, we can multiply the two positions of these primes and obtain the source of light, as is described in Genesis 1:16. Position 12 multiplied by position 21 produces 252, which is the Gematria for light, or luminary.

Light
הַמָּאוֹר

| 200+6+1+40+5 |

252

In Gematria, zeros can be added or removed from a number without changing its intended meaning. Let's add a zero to 252 and obtain 2520. This is the smallest number that is evenly divisible by all nine digits. It is a number much used in the scriptures, both in its plain text, and in its chronology and symbolic language.

$$2520 \div 1 = 2520$$
$$2520 \div 2 = 1260$$
$$2520 \div 3 = 840$$
$$2520 \div 4 = 630$$
$$2520 \div 5 = 504$$
$$2520 \div 6 = 420$$
$$2520 \div 7 = 360$$
$$2520 \div 8 = 315$$
$$2520 \div 9 = 280$$

Genesis 1:1 is the foundation for the remainder of the written Word, and it contains foundation numbers. Its total number value is 2701, which is 37 x 73. The 3 and the 7 are primes, as well as 37 and 73. It is not surprising, then, to find the foundation concept of the whole of God's plan for the salvation and restoration of man, encoded into that first verse. The blood of Jesus Christ which was prophesied, pictured, enacted, and fulfilled – the scarlet thread of redemption – began as a promise in Genesis 1:1 by the encoding of the number 1480 into its Gematria. Using the principle of the Equidistant Letter Sequence (ELS), and counting every 3rd letter and every 7th letter, produces the number 1480, which is the Gematria for the blood of Jesus. as shown in chapter 1. It is the combining of the two codes – the ELS Code and the Number Code – in the very first verse of the Holy Word.

The promise of the slain Lamb was before the foundation of the world, thus it is fitting that its number, 1480, be encoded into the Bible's first verse, before the creation of man. The Apostle Peter told us of this. He said, *"Foreasmuch as ye know that ye were not redeemed with corruptible things, as silver and gold ... but with the precious blood of Christ, as of a lamb without blemish and without spot: who verily was foreordained before the foundation of the world."* (I Peter 1:18-20)

Revelation 13:8 tells of the *"Lamb slain from the foundation of the world."* It was part of the original plan, and was encoded into the basic text which tells us that God (*Elohim*) created the heaven and the earth.

Genesis 1:1 – ELS 3 and ELS 7

(Read from right to left)

earth the		and heaven the			God		created	beginning the	In		
ץ ר א ה	ת א ו	ם י מ ש ה	ת א	ם י ה ל א	א ר ב	ת י ש א ר ב		Totals
90 200 1 5	400 1 6	40 10 40 300 5	400 1	40 10 5 30 1	1 200 2	400 10 300 1 200 2		
200	400	300	1	5	1	1		1
		40		40	2	400		
90		40		40		2		

1480	=	90+200	+	400	+	40	+	300	+	1	+	1	+	40	+	5	+	1	+	2 +400	+	1	Totals

28 THE STONES AND THE SCARLET THREAD

The scarlet thread of redemption that weaves its way through the entire history of man is the precious, innocent blood of Jesus Christ. The Gematria of the scarlet thread is basic to creation and to light. Genesis One is the story of creation, beginning with the creation of light. And we are told in John 1:2 that *"All things were made by Him, and without Him was nothing made."*

In the 8th chapter of Proverbs we have another account of the creation of the earth and man, with one added insight – the love felt and expressed toward man: *"The Lord possessed me in the beginning of his way, before his works of old. I was set up from everlasting, from the beginning, or ever the earth was. When there were no depths, I was brought forth; when there were no fountains abounding with water. Before the mountains were settled, before the hills was I brought forth: while as yet he had not made the earth, nor the fields, nor the highest part of the dust of the world. When he prepared the heavens, I was there: when he set a compass upon the face of the depth: when he established the clouds above: when he strengthened the fountians of the deep: when he gave to the sea his decree, that the waters should not pass his commandment: when he appointed the foundations of the earth: then I was by him, as one brought up with him; and I was daily his delight, rejoicing always before him; rejoicing in the habitable part of his earth; and my delights were with the sons of men."*

His delights were with the sons of men because He knew, even before Adam was created, that man would need a redeemer, and He knew it would be His own innocent blood that would be the price for Adam's sin. *"His delights were with the sons of men."* It was His love for the human

The reason for His gift was love.

family that impelled Him to come to earth and to give His blood in the place of the blood of Adam.

Jesus is, in fact, the very personification of love – and He bears the same number. Jesus is represented by the numbers 1 and 8, the numbers of Beginning and New Beginning. The New Beginning for man can only be a reality because of His love for us. The name of Jesus, in the New Testament, has a number value of 888. It is the triplet of 8s. The Hebrew word that is used throughout the Old Testament meaning love has a number value of 8.

Love
אהב
2 + 5 + 1

8

The creation of man was an act of love, and the redemption of man was an act of love. Love is the life-giving force that links man with his Creator.

The magnitude and greatness of this kind of love is beyond my comprehension, or my ability to describe. However, I would like to share with the reader a little glimpse into the magnificence of that love.

The Apostle John told us that *"In him was life, and the life was the light of men...He was the true Light, which lighteth every man that cometh into the world,"* (John 1:4&9). Yes, He is truly Love and He is truly Light – two life-giving ingredients. Both are represented by light from the sun, engulfing planet earth, man's home. It is not a blind coincidence that light from the sun comes 93 million miles to the earth, and the word "love" in the New Testament, which is always used for God's love, is the word *agape, αγαπη,* which has a number value of 93.

Love
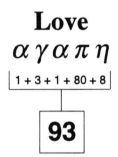

Also, the light, or "brightness" that comes from the sun to our earth bears the number 93. They appear to be intentional numbers.

Brightness
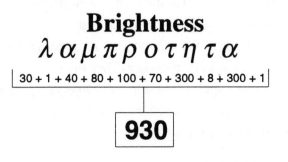

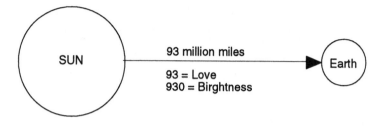

SUN   93 million miles   Earth

93 = Love
930 = Birghtness

With each revolution of the earth on its axis (24 hours), the earth is bathed in light from the sun. A portion of that is also bathed in the reflected light of the sun, from the moon.

With every revolution of our Earth we are literally engulfed in light and love.

We are literally engulfed in light. And, as is indicated by the Gematria, we are also engulfed in love – divine love. It was a love that was willing to die that we might have life.

Apply a little bit of simple arithmatic, and the intent of the numbers is more than just an appearance – it shouts to us with an astounding message!

Convert the 93 million miles to inches. I realize that the 93 million is only a mean, and that the actual distance varies with the elliptical orbit of the earth. But for this calculation, consider the earth's orbit as a circle, with a radius of 93 million miles. Now convert it to inches. And, just as we do in Gematria, we will drop the zeros because it is the base numbers that are important. Then divide that distance by the speed of light. The result is absolutely astounding! It tells us that the light which surrounds and engulfs us is indeed the love of Jesus Christ.

93 x 528 x 12 = 589248

589248 ÷ 186 = 3168

Lord Jesus Christ = 3168

Lord Jesus Christ
Κυριος Ιησους Χριστος

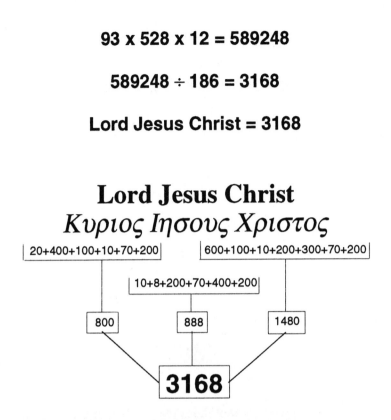

The above calculation is based on the distance that light travels from the sun to our earth, divided by the speed of light. Jesus said, *"I am the light of the world,"* (John 8:12). And that light literally surrounds our earth, bearing His name. Because of this, the next logical step would be to divide the distance that light comes to the earth by the circumference of the earth. Amazingly it produces the number that is the Gematria for Jesus Christ. It looks as if God was intent upon our getting the message. It certainly could not be by coincidence that such a remarkable set of numbers is involved.

$$93 \times 528 \times 12 = 589248$$

$$589248 \div 24883.2 = 2368$$

$$\text{Jesus Christ} = 2368$$

Jesus Christ

$$I \eta \sigma o \upsilon \varsigma \; X \rho \iota \sigma \tau o \varsigma$$

10+8+200+70+400+200	600+100+10+200+300+70+200

888	1480

2368

It is not enough that these two calculations both produce the name of the Lord Jesus Christ. We are completely overwhelmed by yet a third calculation, based on the distance that light travels from the sun to our earth.

The name of Jesus has another spelling, therefore another number. The Greek language spells words differently depending upon their placement in the sentence. It is somewhat similar to our English use of words. For instance, we might spell a word "intent" or we might spell it "intention," yet both have the same meaning. Thus the name of Jesus is sometimes spelled $I\eta\sigma o \upsilon\varsigma$, and sometimes it is spelled $I\eta\sigma o\upsilon$. Both spellings have important Gematria.

Using the same calculation based on the distance that light travels from the sun to our earth, let's now divide it by the mean radius of the earth. We're still dropping the extra zeros, so the mean radius of 3,960 miles will become 396.

93 x 528 x 12 = 589248

589248 ÷ 396 = 1488

Lord Jesus = 1488

Lord Jesus
Κυριος Ιησου

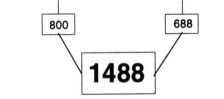

Hold on! We're not through yet. There's more! This amazing calculation, using the distance that light travels from the sun to our earth produces one more number which tells of the Lord Jesus Christ being the Light of the world. It tells of the *"two great lights"* which rule the night and the day – the moonlight being the reflected light of the sun. This time we'll divide by earth's mean diameter, 7,920 miles, and again we'll drop the zero.

$$93 \times 528 \times 12 = 589248$$

$$589248 \div 792 = 744$$

Two great lights = 744

Two great lights

הַמְּאוֹרֹת הַגְּדֹלִים

40+10+30+4+3+5	400+200+6+1+40+5

| 92 | 652 |

744

The two numbers that are the Gematria for "love" in Hebrew and Greek are 8 and 93. We have seen that 93 defines the distance that light travels from the sun to our earth. Multiply 8 times 93 and the product is 744, which is the Gematria for *"two great lights."*

The evidence is overwhelming. It confirms the use of Gematria as a divinely inspired part of the Word of God. The above demonstration is far beyond the possibility of coincidence. It is beautiful and it is exciting, for it tells us of Jesus Christ and the foundation of creation. He is the Foundation (12 x 74 = 888), and He is the Light. His love for the family of Adam is shown by the light that surrounds and engulfs our earth.

A circle with a circumference of 744 will have a diameter of 236.8, which, as has been shown, is the Gematria for Jesus Christ. The evidence is overwhelming. Jesus is truly the *"Light of the world."*

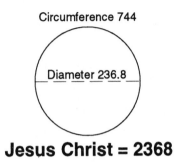

Circumference 744

Diameter 236.8

Jesus Christ = 2368

This relationship of our earth to the sun, and the distance that light travels to us is a foundation principle of the Word of God and the Works of God. As we shall see, as we progress through this study, these foundation truths are clues to the understanding of the Word living, the Word written, the Word in number, the Word in the cosmos, and the Word in stone. We see only pieces, but those small pieces

We are given clues to the Word living, the Word written, the Word in number, the Word in the cosmos, and the Word in stone.

tell us of an Almighty Creator who planned with precision the vast, yet minute, interwoven wonders of His universe and His far-reaching plan for His human family. Our finite minds cannot grasp that which is infinite, but we have been given clues to point the way. Share with me some of those amazing clues.

The light that travels from the sun to our earth comes to us at a speed of 186,000 miles per second. The actual figure is slightly more than that, but this is the accepted rounded figure and apparently the figure used by God in the number patterns. This number is not only basic to earth's relationship to the sun, it is also basic to man's relationship to his Creator.

A square with sides of 186 will have a perimeter of 744. Using that perimeter, and changing it from a square to the circumference of a circle, will produce a circle with a diameter of 2368 (dropping the decimal point). In Psalm 102:25 we read, *"Thou hast laid the foundations of the earth."* That statement, in Hebrew, adds to 744. The concept can be shown graphically by a square with sides of 186, giving a perimeter of 744.

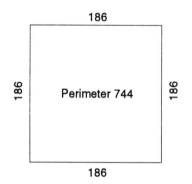

Simply redefine the square as a circle with a circumference of 744, and the diameter of the circle will be 2368, which is the Gematria for the name Jesus Christ.

The number 186 is not only fundamental to the life-giving light that comes to us from the sun, it is also fundamental to the very ground on which we walk.

The earth is composed of magma, or molten rock, within, and solidified, or cooled rock without. 99% of the rock which comprises earth's crust is composed of twelve elements. It is a reminder that 12 is the great foundation number, and it is an integral part of earth's structure. Below are listed these 12 elements in their order of abundance, and beside each element is its atomic number – the number of protons in the nucleus of each. It is not by blind chance that they add to 186. It is part of a master design, prepared by a Master Designer.

Oxygen	8
Silicon	14
Aluminum	13
Iron	26
Calcium	20
Sodium	11
Potassium	19
Magnesium	12
Titanium	22
Phosphorus	15
Hydrogen	1
Manganese	25
	186

This remarkable number – 186 – is found in creation, in light from the sun to our planet, in the earth's crust, in Jesus Christ, in the place of His crucifixion, and all the way to the completed work of His Kingdom. Share with me some of the beauty of this divinely ordained number!

186 = His work (all the work of creation)

186 = Created (I John 1:3)

186 = Everlasting (the beginning of the world, Isaiah 64:4)

186 = According to His image (the creation of man in the image of God)

186 = Firstborn (Jesus, Luke 2:7)

186 = As a tender plant (Jesus, Isaiah 53:2)

186 = Golgotha (the place of Jesus' death)

186 = It is finished (Jesus' words just before He died.)

186 = There shall be no more curse (the completed work of redemption and restoration of man, Revelation 22:3)

The list is impressive! But I would like to add one more important piece of evidence. In the autumn of the year just previous to the spring when Jesus became the antitypical Passover Lamb, Jesus went up to Jerusalem at the time of the Feast of Tabernacles. This was a 7-day feast, followed by a great 8th day. He did not arrive, however, at the beginning of the festival, but rather appeared on the 4th day. On the scale that a thousand years equals one day, we have Jesus arriving on the 4th day – 4000 years. At the last day of the feast, the great 8th day, He stood up and said, *"If any man thirst, let him come unto me and drink,"* (John 7:37). He was speaking prophetically of the world's great 8th day, which immediately follows the 7,000 years, and was telling them the same thing that John would later record in the book of Revelation: *"Let him that is athirst come, and whoso-ever will, let him take the water of life freely,"* (Rev. 22:17).

Israel's feast year began with Passover and ended with the Feast of Tabernacles. There were precisely 186 days from Passover to the great 8th day. The end of that 186 days pictures the end of earth's 7,000-year day, which began with the fall of Adam and ends with the complete

There are 186 days from Passover to the end of the Feast of Tabernacles.

redemption and restoration of all that Adam lost. This is why we find the statement in the book of Revelation: *"And there shall be no more curse."* This statement adds to 186. It fulfills the picture of the 186 days from Passover to the completion of Tabernacles. At the beginning of that great 8th day, the invitation will be given, *"Let him that is athirst come, and whosoever will, let him take the water of life freely."* God's plan for the redemption and restoration of man will be complete.

If we were to read 186 from right to left it would give us 681. In Gematria, numbers can often be read both ways. In this case, it appears to be an intentional use of the number, for the Hebrew words for the last day of the Feast of Tabernacles are האהרון של חג יום טוב, which adds to 681. It is the reverse of the precise count of the number of days from the beginning of their feasts to the last.

It is thus apparent that the number 186 is a foundation upon which His whole plan for man is constructed. It is illustrated by the light (life) that comes to earth from the sun. And the scarlet thread of redemption is woven into it by its number 365, (the scarlet, הַשָּׁנִי = 365). It takes the earth 365 whole days to make one circuit around the sun. If the path of the earth around the sun were a perfect circle, it would have a diameter of 186 million miles. The Creator's choice of distance was not random, it was part of a pattern that includes all of His Works and His Word.

The actual elliptical path of the earth around the sun travels a distance of 595 million miles. A circular path for the earth would travel a distance of a little more than 584 million miles. The elliptical path, in fact, defines a circle. That may sound contradictory and unmathematical, but watch what happens when we consider the length of the elliptical path in feet (dropping the zeros). Multiply 595 million miles by 528 and the product is, surprisingly, our basic principle of π.

$$595 \times 528 = 314,160$$
$$\pi = 3.1416$$

What a marvelous design! It gives us an awareness of the marvelous mind of the Designer. He used an ellipse to show the value of π, when π is actually the key to the geometry of a circle! Perhaps it is telling us that even though the orbital path of the earth around the sun is elliptical, mathematically and symbolically it can be treated as a circle. If so, then let's try treating it as a circle, and observe its magnificent design.

It is not enough that the elliptical orbit of the earth defines π – it also defines ϕ (the Golden Proportion).

The number of whole days that is required for the earth to complete its orbit is 365, the number of the scarlet thread. Divide 365 by π and the result is ϕ. This is astounding!

$$365 \div 3.1416 = 116.18$$
$$\phi = 1:1.618$$

Let me catch my breath! I went back and repeated this calculation several times, just to make sure my calculator was not deceiving me. It's real. It's true!

And, as if the orbit of earth around the sun is not fundamental enough, God has placed the foundation number, 12, in the very relationship of π to ϕ. For this calculation I use ϕ to six decimal places.

$$12 \div \phi \div \phi = (\pi 10)$$
$$\text{or}$$
$$12 \div .618034 \div .618034 = 31.416$$

The above marvelous demonstration of the mind of the Creator shows the link between the earth, sun, light, time, a circle, a square, the Golden Proportion, and the foundation number, 12. All of these play a fundamental role in the tracing of the scarlet thread of redemption through the pages of time.

My friend, Neil Pinter, of Borger, Texas, showed me yet another way in which the circle of the earth relates to the redemptive and saving work of Jesus Christ. He reasoned that if the Greek letter π is the mathematical basis for defining a circle, then its Gematria would probably reflect the same information. The number value of π is 80. In Gematria we can drop the zeros without changing the meaning of the number. Drop the zero and we are left with the number 8. It is the number that represents a New Beginnning through Jesus Christ. The word "save" in Greek has the number value of 8. We have seen that the word "foundation" produces the Gematria of 12 and 74; however, there is yet another Hebrew word for "foundation" (יסוד) which has a number value of 80. With this reasoning in mind, he divided π by π, or 3.14159 ÷ 8 = .392659875. Considering the unit to be the mile, and converting it to inches produces an astonishing figure.

3.14159 ÷ 8 = .392659875
.392659875 x 5280 x 12 = 24,881.392 inches
Circumference of earth = 24,881.392 miles

Impressive indeed! It bears witness to the scarlet thread of redemption that saved Adam and his race from the death penalty. As far as we know, our earth is the only place of salvation in God's creation. These fundamentals of mathematics and Gematria show the circumference of the earth to be clothed with the saving power of Jesus Christ. Just as we found that the distance light travels from the sun to our earth represented His love (8 and 93), so we find that His saving power engulfs our earth. It is a mathematical demonstration of the statement of the Apostle Paul when he said, *"As in Adam all die, so in Christ shall all be made alive,"* (I Cor. 15:22).

The fact of the earth being the place of salvation is demonstrated by its geometry and Gematria. The earth has a mean diameter of 7,920 miles. If we surrounded the earth by a square box, the perimeter of the box would be 31,680 miles. Picture the earth as being completely immersed into the box. The box represents the saving power of the Lord Jesus Christ, whose Gematria is 3168.

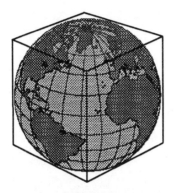

Perimeter of box 31,680 miles
Lord Jesus Christ = 3168

This tells the same story as we have seen demonstrated by the light from the sun bathing the earth in its life-giving power. The earth is the recipient of this light, love and life. It surrounds us and engulfs us. Earth is the *place* of salvation. This, too, is shown by the Gematria. The word "salvation" as it is used in the Hebrew text of the Old Testament, has a number value of 792. The mean diameter of the earth is 7,920 miles. It is not a coincidence. It was planned by a Master Mathematician.

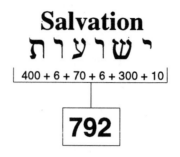

Salvation

ת ו ע ו ש י

400 + 6 + 70 + 6 + 300 + 10

792

As if to impress upon us the importance of the earth being the place of salvation, the Creator also placed salvation's number in earth's radius, 3960 miles.

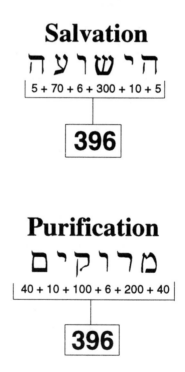

Salvation

ה ע ו ש י ה

5 + 70 + 6 + 300 + 10 + 5

396

Purification

ם י ק ו ר מ

40 + 10 + 100 + 6 + 200 + 40

396

On the Earth

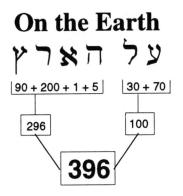

עַל הָאָרֶץ

90 + 200 + 1 + 5		30 + 70
296		100

396

The purification of the earth and of man on the earth is the work of the Kingdom for which Jesus taught us to pray. It will be a time when God's will *"will be done on earth even as it is in heaven."*

The Prophet Isaiah pictured it for us in language that is comforting indeed:

"... until the spirit be poured upon us from on high, and the wilderness be a fruitful field, and the fruitful field be counted for a forest. Then judgment shall dwell in the wilderness, and righteousness remain in the fruitful field. And the work of righteousness shall be peace; and the effect of righteousness quietness and assurance forever. And my people shall dwell in a peaceable habitation, and in sure dwellings, and in quiet resting places."

The means by which this can become a reality for man and the earth, is the shedding of the innocent blood of Jesus Christ. He poured out His life blood to redeem (buy back) Adam and all of Adam's family. When the Roman soldiers came to the cross to hasten the death of the three who had been crucified that afternoon, they found that Jesus was already dead, so they pierced His side with a spear, and His blood poured out upon the ground. It was surety for the promise of the purification of the earth. It legally released the earth from the curse that had been placed upon it by the disobedience of Adam.

The scarlet thread of redemption that had been pictured by the types, illustrations, stories, and human lives throughout the pages of the Old Testament, had now become a legal transaction, signed, sealed and delivered.

3

The Circle and the Scarlet Thread

The blood of Jesus is the scarlet thread that weaves its way through the pages of the Bible. The Gematria for the scarlet thread is indeed an intentional part of the Word. Let's examine its Gematria more closely.

> **360 = Scarlet** (by addition)
> **15 = Scarlet** (by multiplication)
> **365 = The scarlet** (by addition)
> **23 = Thread** (by addition)
> **432 = Thread** (by multiplication)

The first obvious connection to the number 360 is a circle, which has 360 degrees. Other uses of the number 360 in Gematria include: *God; A Garden eastward in Eden; the Lamb's book of life; to shine; sun; the Rock that begat us* (Jesus); *one man should die for the people* (Jesus). Thus we see that the association of 360 is creation, light, redemption and life. One more use of the number 360 is *"Head of the corner,"* which has reference to Jesus Christ as the topstone.

Scarlet, by multiplication, is 15 (when we multiply Gematria we drop the zeros). Other uses of 15 in Gematria are: *Jehovah; God; light; ransom* (blood of Jesus in place of the blood of Adam); *redemption; topstone.*

It becomes obvious that the Gematria of the word "scarlet" has the same meaning, whether we add or multiply.

In the Hebrew text, the word scarlet is preceded by the definite article, which is attached to the beginning of the word, as we would use a prefix in English. It is denoted by the Hebrew letter ה, which has the number value of 5. Thus "the scarlet" adds to 365.

The first association that comes to mind is the 365 whole days in our solar year. It takes the earth 365 whole days to make one orbit of the sun. The number 365 is also the Gematria for *"the foundation of the earth,"* in the Hebrew scriptures. The number is fundamental and foundational – and so is the scarlet thread.

The word "thread" adds to 23. It is the ninth prime number. Nine is the completion of the digits, therefore the number represents wholeness and completion.

Uses of the number 23 in the Gematria of the Bible are interesting indeed, for they speak of life and the Life-Giver, as well as the place of salvation, our earth. Some of the uses of this number are: *living; to give life; to save life; sin offering; brightness; world without end.*

The Gematria of the scarlet thread speaks of life and the Life-Giver.

How interesting that its meaning should include *"world without end,"* for when we multiply "thread" the product is 432, which carries the meaning of the entire world and all that is in it. The number 432 is also fundamental and foundational. Some of its uses in the Gematria of the

Bible are: *foundation; foundation of the earth; habitation; world; all nations; all things; the habitable world.* These uses of 432 tell us the place of salvation – our earth. Other uses of 432 tell us of the One who brings salvation: *the Saviour.* It tells us the place of His birth, *Bethlehem;* the place of His agony, *Gethsemane;* the place of His death, *Jerusalem;* and His purpose in dying, *the Last Adam.*

Habitation

$$\kappa \alpha \tau o \iota \kappa \iota \alpha$$

| 20+1+300+70+10+20+10+1 |

432

World

תבל

| 30+2+400 |

432

All things

$$\pi \alpha \nu \tau \alpha$$

| 80+1+50+300+1 |

432

All Nations

כ ל-ג ו י ם

| 40 x 10 x 6 x 3 x 30 x 20 |

432

The above display of Gematria is evidence of the use of the number 432 pertaining to the earth, man's home. The following display tells of man's redeemer, Jesus, and His work of being the substitute for Adam. It tells of the place of His birth, Bethlehem, and the place of His agony, Gethsemane, and the place of His death, Jerusalem, where He died on a hill called Calvary – giving His innocent blood for the guilty blood of Adam. That hill, just outside the city of Jerusalem, was where Jesus became the "Last Adam."

Saviour

מ ו ש י ע ר

| 6+70+10+300+6+40 |

432

The Branch of Jehovah

צ מ ח י ה ו ה

| 5 x 6 x 5 x 1 x 8 x 40 x 90 |

432

Bethlehem

Βηθλεεμ

| 2 x 8 x 9 x 30 x 5 x 5 x 40 |

432

Gethsemane

Γεθσημανι

| 3 x 5 x 9 x 200 x 8 x 40 x 1 x 50 x 10 |

432

Jerusalem

ירושלם

| 40 x 30 x 300 x 6 x 200 x 10 |

432

Last Adam

εσχατος Αδαμ

| 5x200x600x1x300x70x200 x 1x4x1x40 |

432
(4032)

It has been demonstrated (page 42) that the elliptical path of the earth around the sun can be treated mathematically and symbolically as a circle – a circle of 360° and a circumference of 584 million miles, which the earth traverses in 365 whole days. The diameter of this circle is 186 million miles.

The 360 is the Gematria for "scarlet" and the 365 is the Gematria for "the scarlet." It's relationship to the earth and salvation through Jesus Christ is marvelous. This relationship can be illustrated by a circle and a square. This circular orbit of the earth has a diameter of 186 million miles. Let's draw a square on that diameter, then reshape that square into a circle. Amazingly this new circle will have a diameter of 2368, which is the Gematria for the name Jesus Christ. If that sounds confusing, let's follow this simple illustration:

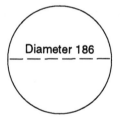

Begin with the circle of earth's orbit. Its diameter will be 186 million miles. Now draw a square on that diameter.

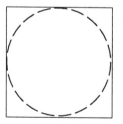

Next, change the square to a circle of the same perimeter. The new, larger circle will have a diameter of 2368. The Gematria of Jesus Christ is 2368.

Jesus Christ = 2368

This simple demonstration reveals the direct relationship of Jesus Christ to the circle of earth's orbit around the sun. We saw previously that the distance light comes from the sun to our earth bears the numbers of His name; and we saw that a box drawn around the earth bears the number of His name. Our earth is literally surrounded by the Gematria of His name. Now we find it is represented in the circle of earth's orbit of the sun.

The use of this principle of the circle and the square can be found over and over again in the Gematria of His Word and in the geometry of His Works

The circle and the square are fundamentally incompatible. The area within a square will never be precisely the same as the area within a circle. This fundamental incompatibility well represents the relationship of fallen man with God. Psalm 90 says *"From everlasting to everlasting thou art God."* His everlastingness – having no beginning nor ending – is represented by a circle, which also has no beginning nor ending. A circle contains the largest area of any closed figure.

A square, on the other hand, is inferior to the circle, and could well represent fallen man.

The ancient Hebrew scriptures tell a most revealing story regarding the first human pair, a man and a woman made in the *"image and likeness"* of God: a human couple, made in perfection. The story reveals the tragic results of their disobedience to their Creator and their fall from that perfection. The penalty placed upon them for their disobedience was death – not immediate death, but a dying existence in which they were estranged from God.

The circle (God) and the square (fallen man) are incompatible because of sin.

But they were given a promise of eventual re-union with their Creator, a return to the oneness they had originally enjoyed. The means by which this re-union could be made possible would be through a redeemer – one to pay the penalty for their disobedience and set them free from their condemnation. Such a redeemer would have to be a substitute, to take their place in death, providing them an opportunity for life. As a surety for the promise of a redeemer, God killed an animal, shedding its innocent blood, and used its skin to clothe them, symbolically covering their sinful condition. This shedding of innocent blood for Adam was the beginning of the tracing of the scarlet thread of redemption through God's whole relationship with man, covering a period of 7,000 years.

The offering of the blood of animals was a picture of the offering of the redemptive blood of Jesus. The real offering of blood for the sin of Adam took place on a hill called Calvary in the year A.D. 33, on the day of Passover, 4,000 years from the day of Adam's sin. This hill was also called Golgotha. The Gematria of these two names for this famous hill reveal the coming together of the circle and the square. And, just as was seen that the circle of relationship between the sun and the earth gives us the fundamental principles of π and ϕ, so the Gematria for Calvary and Golgotha show the re-union of the circle and the square by the use of π and ϕ. The following demonstration of this magnificent re-union is indeed awesome.

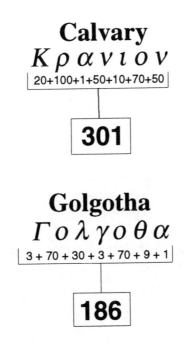

Calvary

$K \rho \alpha \nu \iota o \nu$

20+100+1+50+10+70+50

301

Golgotha

$\Gamma o \lambda \gamma o \theta \alpha$

3 + 70 + 30 + 3 + 70 + 9 + 1

186

For this demonstration, let's begin with a square whose
perimeter is 744, having sides of 186. Project its Golden
Proportion, and the Golden Rectangle that is formed
will have a long side of 301 and a short side of 186.

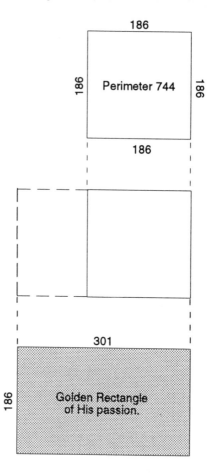

744 = Laid the foundations of the earth
186 = Golgotha
301 = Calvary

301 x ϕ = 186

In Revelation 13:8 Jesus is called the *"Lamb slain from the foundation of the world."* The scarlet thread of redemption was planned long before man was ever created upon this earth. It became a reality on April 3, A.D. 33, on a lonely hill outside Jerusalem – a hill called Calvary (186) and Golgotha (301).

Think of the probabilities that these two names – one being the Golden Proportion of the other – would have been given to this hill by unplanned, blind chance. And think of the probabilities that this event, related to the circle of earth's orbit around the sun, could possibly be by accidental chance. If it be thought merely chance, then let me share with the reader some astounding evidence of its planning by a Master Mathematician.

On pages 42 and 43 was shown the relationship of the orbit of earth to the scarlet thread, to the fundamental relationship of a circle, π, and the fundamental relationship of the Golden Proportion, ϕ. Let's review it brifely.

The earth makes one complete orbit of the sun in 365 whole days. The Gematria for "the scarlet" is 365. The number 365 divided by π produces ϕ. These are basic fundamentals of physics and mathematics.

$$365 \div 3.14159 = 116.18$$
$$\pi = 3.14159$$
$$\phi = 1:1.618$$

The π relationship is seen by the 360° of a circle and the number 360 as the Gematria for "scarlet." It is also seen in the circular orbit of earth around the sun, which is a circumference of 584 million miles, taking 365 whole days.

The ϕ relationship is seen by the fact of Golgotha (186) being the Golden Proportion of Calvary (301).

As shown in chapter 1, the number 148 is interwoven into the story of the scarlet thread, bringing us to the offering of Jesus on Calvary. When Judah's twin sons were being born, the first put forth his hand and the midwife tied on it a scarlet thread. We saw that the Gematria for this was 1480. Then we saw that the Passover – the killing of the lamb and the sprinkling of its blood on the doorframes of the houses – not only pictured the offering of Jesus Christ, and His blood being shed for Adam, but the Gematria of Passover (148), blood (148), corresponded perfectly with the Gematria of Christ (1480) and the number of years (1,480) between the first Passover and the fulfillment at Golgotha (186). Now observe how these numbers relate to the orbit of earth around the sun.

Begin with the circular orbit of earth around the sun. It would be a distance of 584 million miles. This would be accomplished in 365 whole days.

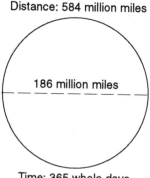

Distance: 584 million miles

186 million miles

Time: 365 whole days

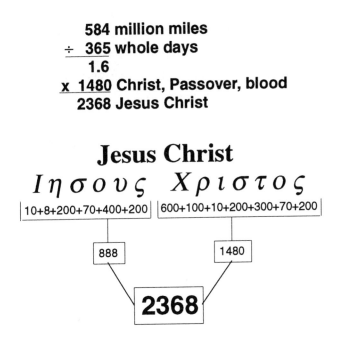

$$584 \text{ million miles}$$
$$\div\ 365 \text{ whole days}$$
$$1.6$$
$$\times\ 1480 \text{ Christ, Passover, blood}$$
$$2368 \text{ Jesus Christ}$$

Jesus Christ

$$I\ \eta\ \sigma\ o\ \upsilon\ \varsigma\qquad X\ \rho\ \iota\ \sigma\ \tau\ o\ \varsigma$$

| 10+8+200+70+400+200 | 600+100+10+200+300+70+200 |

888   1480

2368

There is no way that these relationships could be by blind, unplanned, chance. They are a marvelous demonstration of a master design, planned by a Master Designer. It is the evidence of the scarlet thread of redemption that was woven into the history of man, long before that history even began. It was history written in advance. And it was fulfilled precisely on time, on the afternoon of Passover, April 3, in the year A.D. 33.

Can we have confidence in the prophetic word of the Bible? Can we rest in the assurance that all that God has promised will actually come to pass? I believe the above demonstration of His pre-planning can certainly give us confidence that His plan for the redemption of man will not fail – that it will all be fulfilled precisely as He has planned.

Jesus Christ did indeed shed the redemptive blood precisely on time – a time that was planned from the beginning. It provided for the restoration of all that was lost in Adam. That restoration is the work of earth's great Millennium. The redemption has already been fulfilled, thus we can have the positive assurance that the restoration will be fulfilled exactly as prophesied, and precisely on time.

4

A Circle of Stones

The story of the Hebrew people in the Old Testament is a fascinating one. Students of the Old Testament find in the experiences of those people many prophetic illustrations. Many of the things that God instructed them to do had a deeper meaning than may have appeared to the people at the time. One such story was the crossing of the Jordan River.

The Israelites, under the leadership of Moses, fled from Egyptian bondage and wandered as nomads, without a land, for a period of forty years. After the death of Moses, their newly appointed leader, Joshua, was instructed by God to bring the people across the Jordan and into the land that had been promised to them for a possession.

God instructed Joshua to appoint twelve men, one from each tribe, to take a stone from the middle of the Jordan and bring it to shore on the west bank. These were no small stones, for the instruction was for each man to carry it upon his shoulder.

The stones were carried to a small hill and there placed in a circle. They were to be for a memorial of their deliverance from Egypt, from their homeless wandering in the wilderness, and the miraculous crossing of the Jordan on dry land.

"And Joshua said unto them, Pass over before the Ark of the Lord your God into the midst of the Jordan, and take you up every man a stone upon his shoulder, according to the number of the tribes of the children of Israel: that this may be a sign among you, that when your children ask their fathers in time to come, saying, What mean ye by these stones? Then ye shall answer them, that the waters of Jordan were cut off before the Ark of the Covenant of the Lord; when it passed over Jordan, the waters of the Jordan were cut off: and these stones shall be for a memorial unto the children of Israel forever ... that all the people of the earth might know the hand of the Lord, that it is mighty; that ye might fear the Lord your God forever." (Joshua 4:5-24)

The twelve stones of Gilgal were placed in a circle, as a memorial.

"And the Lord said unto Joshua, This day have I rolled away the reproach of Egypt from off you. Wherefore the name of the place is called Gilgal unto this day." (Joshua 5:9)

That statement was a play on words, which is quite often found in the Old Testament record. The word Gilgal literally means a wheel or that which is circular, but it was also used to mean "rolling away," or a "whirlwind." Thus the rolling away of the reproach of Egypt, and the placing of the stones in a circle as a wheel, appropriately gave the place the name of Gilgal.

The twelve stones of Gilgal remained as a memorial for over 2,000 years. Jerome, once known as the "Patron saint of Christian and ecclesiastical learning," mentioned that the site of the camp of Gilgal and the twelve stones was still distinguishable in his day (4th century A.D.). He said it was about two miles from Jericho. By the 7th century A.D. a church had been built at the site, but the stones were said to still stand.

In the Septuagint, the Greek text of the Old Testament, the name Gilgal is τα Γαλγαλα, which has a number equivalent of 370.

Gilgal

τα Γαλγαλα

300+1+3+1+30+3+1+30+1

370

As was shown on page 25, the number 37 is the 12th prime. The placing of these 12 stones whose number is 37 was not simply a random happening. God instructed Joshua to construct this circle of stones because it had importance in the story of redemption.

The evidence reveals that the twelve stones of Gilgal were to be not only a memorial of the event of the Israelites crossing the Jordan and entering Canaan, but also a most fitting prophetic illustration of the deliverance of the faithful Christian from death and into the heavenly Kingdom. That deliverance comes through the shed blood of Jesus Christ. He is the foundation upon which redemption and restoration can become an accomplished fact.

We saw in chapter 2 that the foundation numbers are 12 and 74. By multiplying these two foundation numbers we obtain the number of the name of Jesus – 888. He is represented by the number 8, the number of New Beginning. The number 37 is the highest prime factor of 74, the foundation number. 37 is, in fact, a prime factor in nearly all of the names and titles of Jesus. (In my book *Jesus Christ: the Number of His Name,* I list 194 of those names and titles which are multiples of 37.)

The number 37 beautifully represents the wholeness of the person and work of Jesus. Both the Hebrew word for "whole" and the Greek word for "whole" as used in the Old and New Testaments, add to 370. It is a basic concept.

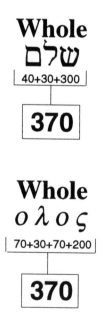

Whole

שלם

40+30+300

370

Whole

ο λ ο ς

70+30+70+200

370

The concept of wholeness is pictured by a circle – that which has no beginning nor ending, continuing forever in perfection. Thus the Gematria for Gilgal – 37 – is profound!

The circle of Gilgal contained 12 stones, one for each of the twelve tribes of Israel.

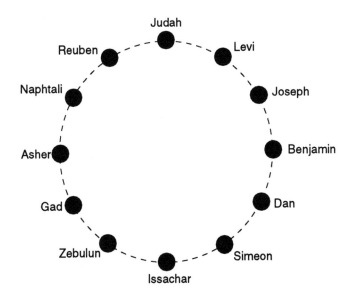

The dimensions of the circle are not given. Neither are the names ascribed to each stone. We are only told that there was a stone for each of the twelve tribes. We know that the tribe of Joseph was divided between his two sons, Ephraim and Manassah, thus creating thirteen tribes. We also know that the listing of the twelve tribes in the book of Revelation eliminates Dan and places Manassah in his stead. However, I have shown the circle with the names of the original twelve sons of Jacob.

About 832 years after this event, the twelve names are listed again as describing the name of each gate in the city that the prophet Ezekiel saw in vision, and the original names of Jacob's twelve sons are given. Interestingly, Ezekiel saw them as describing each side of a square – three gates on each side. Ezekiel gave us the dimensions of the square.

"It was round about eighteen thousand measures (cubits): *and the name of the city from that day shall be 'The Lord is There.'"* (Ezekiel 48:35)

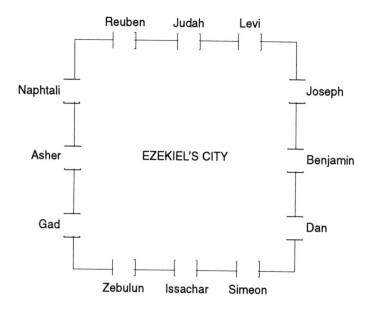

The unit of measure was a very special one that God gave to Ezekiel. He said it would be *"a cubit and a hand-breadth,"* and was to be called a *"Great Cubit."* The cubit in use at that time was called the "moderate cubit," which, stated in our terms would be 18+ inches; and the handbreadth was slightly more than 3 inches. When converted, it would measure 1.76 feet. Thus the measure around the perimeter of the square city would be 31,680 feet, bearing the number of the Lord Jesus Christ, 3168. Each side would measure 7,920 feet, corresponding to the 7,920 miles in the mean diameter of the earth. A remarkable square, indeed! It conveys the meaning of being earth-commensurate, and bears the number of the One who came to earth to bring salvation to Adam's race.

Since the Gilgal circle and Ezekiel's City bear the same names – one being a circle and the other a square – let's combine them into a harmonious unit, bearing the same numbers.

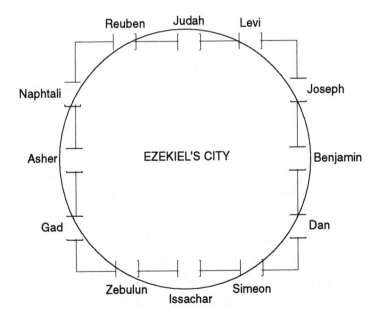

Perimeter of square city = 31,680 feet
Circumference of Gilgal circle = 316.8 inches
Lord Jesus Christ = 3168

Of course we have not been given the actual dimensions of the Gilgal circle. The above is only a supposition based on its relationship to the known dimensions of other circles and squares. This suggested measurement for Gilgal gives it a diameter of 8.4 feet, which appears to be a reasonable assumption, based on the fact of twelve stones that were so large the men had to carry them on their shoulders. Such stones would probably be about 12 inches in diameter. This is, of course, only a guess, based on the awareness of what one man can carry on his shoulder. Thus it would build a circle of stones with about 14.4 inches of space between them.

We do know, however, that the circle was divided into 12 sections of 30° each. Surprisingly, there is another ancient stone circle, still in existence today, whose circumference is divided into 30 sections of 12° each. And this one can be measured because it is still there. It is the outer circle of stones at the monument called Stonehenge, in England. This circle of stones has been named the Sarsen Circle, because the stones are of sarsen, a kind of natural sandstone.

Stonehenge was built over 500 years *before* the Gilgal circle was constructed. Its divisions of 30 sections of 12° each causes one to wonder about the possibility of other similarities. So let's measure the Sarsen Circle.

Many archaeologists have carefully measured everything at Stonehenge. The Sarsen Circle has been found to have a mean circumference of 316.8 feet. Wow! That's the same number as was found in the perimeter of Ezekiel's city. That's the same number for the perimeter of a square drawn around the circle of the earth. And it is the same

The Sarsen Circle at Stonehenge has a mean circumference of 316.8 feet.

number I have suggested for the mean circumference of Gilgal. It is the Gematria for Lord Jesus Christ, 3168.

Now, wait a minute! What does Stonehenge have to do with all of this. Is it mentioned in the Bible too? Is it part of the weaving of the scarlet thread? Why would its prominent stone circle, still in existence today, bear the number of the Lord Jesus Christ? They are questions worth pursuing.

Stonehenge is one of our most ancient monuments still in existence today. It stands unique among all the stone monuments of ancient man. Historians, archaeologists, astronomers, and the just plain curious have sought for centuries to solve its mysteries. What is it, and why is it still there?

Today it has become a popular tourist attraction, located on the Salisbury Plain just southwest of London, England. So popular, in fact, that it has become necessary to forbid the public entrance in the interests of preserving the stones. Unfortunately, unthinking tourists like to take samples and souvenirs home, and they like to climb upon the stones, wearing them down. Thus a fence has been built, keeping destructive hands and feet off the priceless ancient stones.

Has this stone monument, which was in existence during the days of the writing of the books of the Old Testament, been mentioned by any of its writers? Do we have any legitimate reason to think it might be a part of the weaving of the scarlet thread, other than the fact of its remarkable dimensions?

The prophet Jeremiah was aware that there were "witnesses" in the earth that would be called "signs and wonders." He said: *The Great, the Mighty God, the Lord of Hosts is his name ... who has set signs and wonders in the land of Egypt, even unto this day, and in Israel, and among other men,"* (Jer. 32:19, 20).

There is ample evidence that the *"sign and wonder"* in the land of Egypt is the Great Pyramid; and there is also ample evidence that the "sign and wonder" in the land of Israel is Solomon's Temple; but what about among other men? Was he, in fact, referring to Stonehenge? Jeremiah stated it in the past tense – *"has set signs and wonders"* – and we know that all three of these structures had been built before his day, and were still in existence.

Let's take a look at Stonehenge and see if it appears to be one of those *"signs and wonders."*

On the opposite page is a ground plan of Stonehenge. It consists of several concentric circles, some of stone, and some of earth. The stone circles occupy the central portion, and they are surrounded by a circle of 56 holes, which in turn is surrounded by an earth bank, which is finally sur-

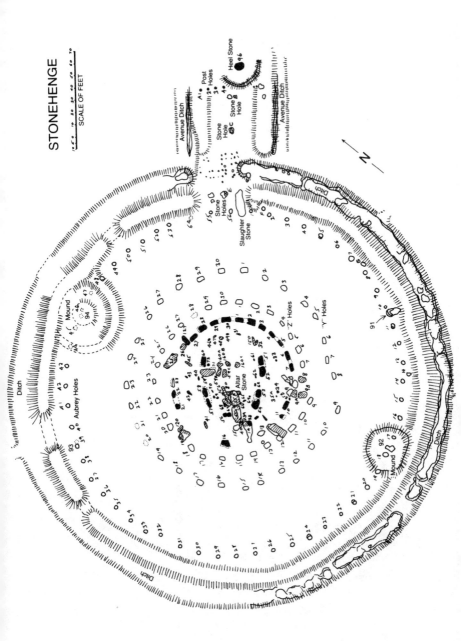

STONEHENGE

SCALE OF FEET

N

Avenue Ditch

Avenue Ditch

A · Post
· Holes

Heel Stone
96

Stone
Hole B

Stone
Hole
C

Stone
Holes

Slaughter
Stone

Z Holes

Y Holes

Ditch

Ditch

Mound
94

Mound
92

Aubrey Holes

93

Altar
Stone

16

Ditch

A CIRCLE OF STONES 73

rounded by a ditch.

The outer circle of stones, which is toward the center of the drawing, consisted of 30 upright stones, connected at the top by 30 lintels, giving the circle stability. The lintels formed a continuous perfect circle. Some of the stones are missing today, and are thus not shown. The circle of uprights has, in modern times, been named the Sarsen Circle. The 30 uprights were placed around the circle at 12° intervals.

Immediately within the Sarsen Circle stands a circle of smaller stones, known today as the Bluestone Circle. They are of a much different geological formation than the sarsen stones, being "eruptive rocks," known in geology as dolerite and rhyolite. The dimensions and geometric relationship of these two stone circles is amazing. They are earth-commensurate.

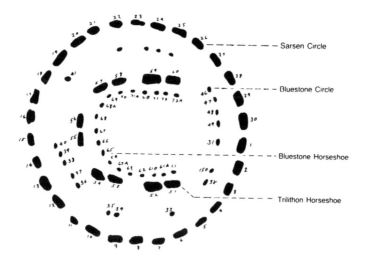

The relationship of the Sarsen Circle to the Bluestone Circle is identical to the relationship of the earth to a square drawn on its circumference. If the Sarsen Circle were re-defined as a square, the Bluestone Circle would fit within it, touching on all four sides.

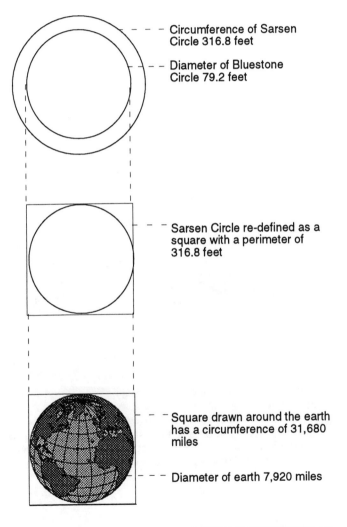

Circumference of Sarsen Circle 316.8 feet

Diameter of Bluestone Circle 79.2 feet

Sarsen Circle re-defined as a square with a perimeter of 316.8 feet

Square drawn around the earth has a circumference of 31,680 miles

Diameter of earth 7,920 miles

Bear in mind that this most remarkable set of stone circles was built during the lifetime of Shem. The tourist who visits Stonehenge today, does not see this relationship of its Bluestone Circle to the dimensions of our earth because many of the stones are missing, and some are lying on their sides. Below is an artist's conception of Stonehenge at its completion, 4,000 years ago, based on the evidence provided by archaeologists who have measured and mapped it. Even in its original condition, it is not easily discerned that it is earth-commensurate.

The upper surface of the circle of lintels connecting the tops of the uprights on the Sarsen Circle are level with gavity, while the ground below actually slopes toward the Avon river. This remarkable feature suggests that Stonehenge should properly be viewed from above. Thus the relationship of the Sarsen Circle to the Bluestone Circle would be more apparent.

But let's take a closer look. That Sarsen Circle is truly remarkable. It is not only earth-commensurate in its dimensions, it clearly bears the number of the Lord Jesus Christ, 3168. And if we were to compute the area within its mean circumference, we'd find that it contains 888 square yards. As previously observed, the name Jesus has a Gematria of 888. The measure around the outer face of these stones is 331.7 feet, producing a diameter of 105.6 feet. How beautiful, for He is the One who brings salvation – and the Hebrew letters which spell *"The joy of thy salvation,"* (Psalm 51:12), has a Gematria of 1056.

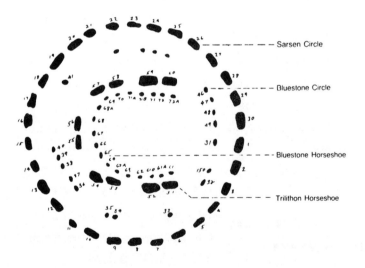

This amazing ancient circle of stones, just like the path of earth's orbit, is a repository for π. But, one might ask, aren't all circles a demonstration of π? Perhaps, but not like this one.

Remember, on page 42 it was shown that the elliptical path of the earth around the sun, converted to feet, would bear the number 314,160 followed by many zeros which we dropped. It demonstrated that the Creator used the true elliptical path of the earth to represent a circle.

$$595 \times 528 = 314,160$$
$$\pi = 3.1416$$

Now we find that π is also represented by the number and placement of the stones of the Sarsen Circle. And it is tied to the square city that Ezekiel saw in vision. God had given to Ezekiel a new unit of measure – the Great Cubit. Then he gave to Ezekiel a measuring reed, which was six Great Cubits in length. If we used this measuring reed to measure the Sarsen Circle it would produce something most exciting.

The number of reeds in the circumference of the outer face of the Sarsen Circle is 31.4159, or 10 times π. And, as

The outer face of the Sarsen Circle defines π

if to emphasize the importance of that amazing circle to the π value, and to the British Mile, we find that the area within this outer face is .000314159 of a square mile.

If the circle of 30 stones has an outer circumference of 31.4159 reeds, then each segment of three stones would measure π.

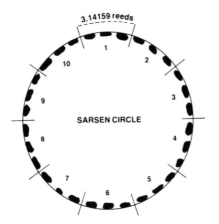

3.14159 reeds

1 2 3 4 5 6 7 8 9 10

SARSEN CIRCLE

This relationship of Ezekiel's square city to the ancient circle of stones at Stonehenge is not simply a coincidence. It gives evidence of being part of a pattern – a pattern of pictures and events that are all tied together by the scarlet thread of redemption.

Coming down through history, from the time that Ezekiel was given the vision of the square city to about A.D. 90 - 96, we find the Apostle John exiled on the Isle of Patmos. While alone in exile, he received a vision of a future city. He called it the New Jerusalem. It is described by John as a cube, with a ground plan of twelve thousand furlongs per side, which would compute to 7,920,000 feet per side, multiplied

The perimeter of the New Jerusalem is 316,800,000 feet.

by 4 would produce a perimeter of 316,800,000 feet. These numbers, by now, are our old friends. They are not random numbers, nor is it simply a coincidence that John recorded these dimensions. It is part of a magnificent plan, designed by the Creator Himself.

And, just as Ezekiel's city had three gates on each side, making twelve in all, bearing the names of the twelve tribes of Israel, so we find the same with the New Jerusalem. The repetition of the design confirms that it has meaning, and was not just the ramblings of an ancient seer.

When John heard the names of the twelve tribes of Israel (Revelation 7), he did not hear the same list that Ezekiel heard, yet the design was identical. The list which John heard placed Manassah instead of Dan. Probably the reason for this is because of the prophecy of Jacob, at the time when he was dying, in which he told what the future of each of his twelve sons would be *"in the last days,"* (Genesis 49:1). He had prophesied that Dan would be *"a serpent by the way, an adder in the path, that biteth the horse heels, so that his rider shall fall backward."* Because of this, some students of end-time prophecy suggest that it will be a person whose lineage is from Dan that will become the instrument of Satan in the last days. The meaning of the name Dan is *"judged."*

This may well be true. However, it is also interesting that by making this one change in the list, the Gematria takes on amazing significance. The total of their names bears the same number as Jesus, with the elimination of the zero. There is no way this could be a random coincidence. It was the work of a Master Mathematician, who formed a plan for eternity. These twelve gates on the New Jerusalem bear the name of Jesus, whose name means "Salvation."

Spelling these names the way they are given in Thayers

Greek Lexicon, their total is found to be 8880.

Judah	*Ιουδα*	**485**
Reuben	*Ρουβην*	**630**
Gad	*Γαδ*	**8**
Asher	*Ασηρ*	**309**
Nepthalim	*Νεφθαλειμ*	**650**
Manasses	*Μανασσης*	**700**
Simeon	*Συμεων*	**1495**
Levi	*Λευι*	**445**
Issachar	*Ισσαχαρ*	**1112**
Zebulon	*Ζαβουλων*	**1360**
Joseph	*Ιωσηφ*	**1518**
Benjamin	*Βενιαμιν*	**168**
		8880

Jesus = 888
Salvation of our God (Isa. 52:10) = 888

These twelve gates to the New Jerusalem bear the number of salvation through Jesus. John said: *"And the gates of it shall not be shut at all by day: for there shall be no night there. And they shall bring the glory of the nations into it. And there shall in no wise enter into it anything that defileth, neither whatsoever worketh abomination, or maketh a lie: but they which are written in the Lamb's book of life."* (Revelation 21:25-27)

This city, with its perimeter bearing the name of the Lord Jesus Christ (3168) has twelve gates on that perimeter, whose Gematria represents Jesus (888) and the salvation which He brings to the family of Adam.

I stand in awe of this amazing demonstration of the authenticity of Gematria in the Word of God. It took the mind of God to plan such intricacies. When Jacob named

The naming of Jacob's twelve baby boys was part of the scarlet thread of redemption. his twelve sons, little did he know that their names would be posted at the entrances to the New Jerusalem, and their numbers would spell salvation through Jesus Christ, in a language which did not then exist. It becomes obvious that the naming of those twelve baby boys was the work of God, and was a part of the weaving of the scarlet thread of redemption. This same obvious analogy applies to the naming of Joseph's two sons, Ephraim and Manasseh.

Because the dimensions of the New Jerusalem and the names on the gates bear such outstanding significance, it caused me to look further into the description of this marvelous city, given by John. Its numbers are magnificent!

John not only described a city that *"lieth foursquare,"* but he also said it had a high wall of 144 cubits. We can picture a square city having a wall within it, but it is a little more difficult to place a wall within a cube. What was John describing? And why did he specifically call it a *"wall great and high."* And why were the dimensions of the city given in furlongs and the dimensions of the wall in cubits?

The first thing that comes to mind is the fact that 144 is one of the code numbers in the Gematria of the Bible. This number always describes that which is in God's realm – the realm of righteousness – as opposed to that which is in Satan's realm which is unrighteousness.

Using the two units, furlongs and cubits, we find something positively remarkable! The dimensions of the New Jerusalem are geometrically the same as the two outer stone circles of Stonehenge – the Sarsen Circle and the Bluestone Circle. The similarity is in the numbers and the difference is in the scale, or units

The New Jerusalem is geometrically identical to the Sarsen Circle and the Bluestone Circle of Stonehenge.

used. But we just saw that these two circles at Stonehenge use precisely the same numbers as the circle of the earth within a square. Thus the New Jerusalem, like Stonehenge, is also earth-commensurate.

When we compute the perimeter of the square of the ground plan of the New Jerusalem, we realize that a circle that would fit within it would have a circumference of 14,400,000 whole royal cubits. John simply dropped the zeros, just as we do in Gematria. This leads to the obvious conclusion that John was describing a circular wall within the square city. But the city was not only square, it was cubical. So how do we fit a circular wall within a cube? The very fact that John described it as *"great and high"* suggests that it may have completely filled the cube, which would, in three dimensions, be a sphere.

Visualizing the New Jerusalem as a sphere within a cube we can easily see its similarity to the sphere of the earth within a cube, as shown on page 45. The two stone circles at Stonehenge are the same representation in two dimensions. All three use the same numbers, but to different scales, just as John used different scales when describing the square city (furlongs) and the circular wall (cubits).

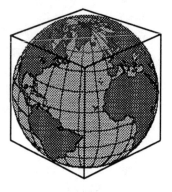

Earth
Diameter 7,920 miles
Perimeter of square 31,680 miles
Lord Jesus Christ = 3168

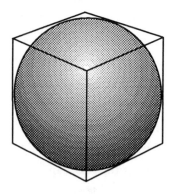

New Jerusalem
Diameter of wall 7,920,000 feet
Perimeter of square 31,680,000 feet
Lord Jesus Christ = 3168

The two outer stone circles at Stonehenge – Sarsen Circle and Bluestone Circle – bear this identical relationship in two dimensions, but yet a different scale. Below is a diagram showing the New Jerusalem superimposed over Stonehenge.

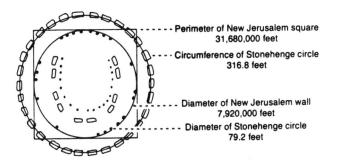

Perimeter of New Jerusalem square
31,680,000 feet

Circumference of Stonehenge circle
316.8 feet

Diameter of New Jerusalem wall
7,920,000 feet

Diameter of Stonehenge circle
79.2 feet

These earth-commensurate numbers also bear the numbers of the Lord Jesus Christ. The visual symbolism depicts the New Jerusalem engulfing the earth. And, indeed, this is the way John described it – as coming down out of heaven to the earth. *"And he carried me away in the spirit to a great and high mountain, and showed me that great city, the holy Jerusalem, descending out of heaven from God,"* (Revelation 21:10)

Just as Gilgal was a circle of stones, each bearing a name of one of the tribes of Israel, so the wall of the New Jerusalem has twelve foundation stones, each bearing the name of one of the twelve apostles. But unlike the Gilgal circle, this circle of stones that John saw in vision was made of precious stones – each one a thing of beauty.

"And the wall of the city had twelve foundations, and in them the names of the twelve apostles of the Lamb.... And the foundations of the wall of the city were garnished with all manner of precious stones," (Revelation 21:14 & 19).

The names of these twelve apostles, exactly as they appear in Thayer's Greek Lexicon are as follows, with their Gematria:

Peter	Πετρος	755
Andrew	Ανδρεας	361
James	Ιακωβος	1103
John	Ιωαννης	1119
Philip	Φιλιππος	980
Nathanael	Ναθαναηλ	150
Levi (Matthew)	Λευι	445
Thomas	Θωμας	1050
James (son of Alpheus)	Ιακωβος Αλφαιου	2115
Lebbaeus (Thaddeus)	Λεββαιος	320
Simon the Canaanite	Σιμων ο κανανιος	1573
Judas	Ιουδας	685
		10656

10656 ÷ 12 = 888

Jesus = 888

Salvation of our God (Isa. 52:10) = 888

Some have questioned why Judas should appear in this list. Why not the Apostle Paul? I don't know for sure. But just as the Gilgal circle of stones included Dan, so the New Jerusalem circle of precious stones includes Judas. In each case they were part of the original twelve.

The striking similarity lies in the circle and the square. The circle of Gilgal is superimposed by the square of Ezekiel's city. The Stonehenge circles are superimposed by the New Jerusalem. And the New Jerusalem is composed of a square enclosing a circle. It is not likely a blind coincidence. It has the appearance of specific planning by a Great Designer.

The twelve precious stones of the foundation circle of the New Jerusalem were named as to the kind of stone. Using the names exactly as they are spelled in Thayer's Greek Lexicon, we find their Gematria also apparently intentional.

Jasper	ιασπις	501
Sapphire	σαπφειρος	1166
Chalcedony	Χαλκηδων	1513
Emerald	σμαραγδος	619
Sardonyx	σαρδονυξ	885
Sardius	σαρδιον	435
Chrysolyte	Χρυσολιθος	1689
Beryl	βηρυλλος	840
Topaz	τοπαζος	728
Chrysophrasus	Χρυσοπρασος	2021
Jacinth	υακινθινος	820
Amethyst	αμεθυστος	1225
		12442

These were the foundation stones of the wall. The dimensions of the wall, as John recorded, were 144 cubits. John dropped the zeros, because if we compute it we find it actually would have been 14,400,000 whole royal cubits. However, we'll drop the zeros, just like John did, and divide the total Gematria for the foundation gemstones by 144.

$$12442 \div 144 = 86.4$$

The New Jerusalem was described as a cube, with each side measuring 12,000 furlongs. This would mean that the square measure of each side would be 144,000,000 square furlongs. A cube has six sides. Multiply this figure by 6 and the total square surface area of the cube is 864,000,000 square furlongs. It is amazing that the Gematria for the gemstones of the foundation should relate so perfectly to the square measure of the cube. And why not, for the name Jerusalem bears the number 864.

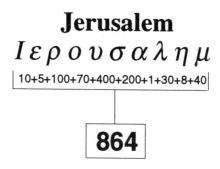

Jerusalem
$I \varepsilon \rho o \upsilon \sigma \alpha \lambda \eta \mu$
| 10+5+100+70+400+200+1+30+8+40 |

864

These twelve foundation gemstones bore the names of each of the original twelve apostles, Their arrangement was circular. This arrangement is identical to the Gilgal circle of stones which bore the names of the original twelve tribes of Israel. Using the Gematria for the gemstones, and dividing by π (because we are dealing with a circle), we find the result would be 3960. It bears the number of "salvation." And indeed the New Jerusalem is all about salvation.

$$12442 \div \pi = 3960$$

Salvation

הי שׁועה

| 5+70+6+300+10+5 |

396

The scarlet thread of redemption has woven its way through the pages of time, from its beginnings in the Garden of Eden to the ultimate reality of the New Jerusalem. It is the story of salvation. It began when Adam sinned, and lost his righteousness before God, and in order to cover Adam's unrighteousness, God killed an animal, shedding its innocent blood, that He might clothe Adam with its skin. The story progressed to the shedding of the blood of an innocent animal by Abel, as he sacrificed one from his flock as an offering to God. It continued with the offering of a ram in the place of Isaac, on Mount Moriah. The scarlet thread of redemption was again enacted by the killing of the Passover lamb on the night the Israelites fled from Egypt. Precisely 1,480 years later, the true Passover Lamb, Jesus Christ, shed His innocent blood on a hill then called Calvary – it was part of the same hill once called Moriah. And now we see its fulfillment in the New Jerusalem, which engulfs man's home, earth, with its salvation and restoration. The story covers a period of 7,000 years.

John saw the fulfillment of this in his vision. He described it thus:

"And I, John, saw the holy city, New Jerusalem, coming down from God out of heaven, prepared as a bride adorned for her husband. And I heard a great voice out of heaven saying, Behold, the tabernacle of God is with men, and he will dwell with them, and they shall be his people, and God himself shall be with them, and be their God. And God shall wipe away all tears from their eyes; and there shall be no more death, neither sorrow, nor crying, neither shall there be any more pain; for the former things are passed away." (Revelation 21:2-4)

John described it as coming down and engulfing the earth. And indeed we have observed that its dimensions are precisely the same as the earth, but to a different scale. This is the *"new earth"* that has been promised to man. It has all been made possible by the shedding of the innocent blood of Jesus Christ, redeeming Adam and his race.

Scarlet has a Gematria of 360, the same as the number of degrees in a circle. The complete circle of gemstones has a total Gematria of 12442. If this number represents the circle, then dividing by 360 would give the number represented by each degree of the circle – 34.56.

$$12442 \div 360 = 34.56$$

This is a number that has great significence in the Gematria of the Bible. It pertains to God's completed work of the redemption and restoration of man. John recorded the words of Jesus (Revelation 3:12) regarding the city called the New Jerusalem: *"Him that overcometh ... I will write upon him the name of my God, and the name of the city of my God, which is New Jerusalem, which cometh down out of heaven from my God."* This city bears the number 3456.

City of my God
τῆς πόλεως τοῦ Θεοῦ μου

300+8+200+80+70+30+5+800+200

300+70+400+9+5+70+400+40+70+400

3456
(3457)

This number, 3456, defines the work of the Kingdom in bringing its blessings of life and peace to man. It represents the dominion of Jesus Christ as the King on David's throne. It also represents the great antitypical Feast of Tabernacles – the final festival of the Hebrew sacred year, which was a time of rejoicing and celebration of God's blessings. And this is what is shown by the Gematria of 3456.

3456 = His dominion, ממשלתו,
(Psalm 145:13) (by multiplication)
3456 = His kingdom, מלכותו,
(Psalm 103:22) (by multiplication)
3456 = The Feast of Tabernacles, חג הסכות,
(Zechariah 14:18) (by multiplication)

The righteousness and peace of that Kingdom, under the administration of Jesus Christ, will be world-wide in its scope.

"And it shall come to pass, that every one that is left of all the nations which came against Jerusalem shall even go up from year to year to worship the King, the Lord of hosts, and to keep the feast of tabernacles," (Zechariah 14:18).

Multiply the digits in 3456 and we find it is the number of degrees in a circle, and it is the Gematria for "scarlet." The Mathematician who designed it is marvelous!

3 x 4 x 5 x 6 = 360
Scarlet = 360
Degrees in a circle – 360

The circular wall of the New Jerusalem, with its twelve

gemstones, each bearing the name of one of the original twelve apostles, is, in three dimensions, a sphere which is enclosed on six sides by a cube. Each side of the cube is 144,000,000 square furlongs. A cube has 6 sides, thus its entire square surface measures 864,000,000 square furlongs. This number is reflected in the Gematria of the gemstones of the circular wall. The total of its Gematria is 12442. Divide this by the measure of the wall – 144 cubits, and the product is 86.4. It is part of a magnificent pattern, designed from the beginning!

$$12442 \div 144 = 86.4$$
$$144 \times 6 = 864$$
$$God = 864$$

God
Θεων
| 9+5+800+50 |

864

"Then cometh the end, when he shall have delivered up the kingdom to God, even the Father ...for he (Jesus) must reign till he hath put all enemies under his feet. The last enemy that shall be destroyed is death ... and when all things shall be subdued unto him, then shall the Son also

himself be subject unto him that put all things under him, that God may be all in all." (I Corinthians 15:24-28)

The beautiful plan for the salvation and restoration of man will have come full circle – from God who designed and planned it, back to Him. It is the complete circle of His plan of redemption, woven through the history of man by the scarlet thread – the blood of Jesus Christ.

5
The Great Pyramid and Stonehenge

The Great Pyramid is the oldest wonder of the ancient world, and the only one still in existence today. However, modern research has also shown that the ancient stone circles, known today as Stonehenge, should also be counted as one of the ancient wonders of the world.

These two stone wonders have come down to us through more than 4,000 years of man's history, and although vandals have attempted to alter and even destroy them, they still stand mute through the ages, hiding their secrets and inspiring historians, philosophers, archaeologists, theologians, and the just plain curious to search for their meanings and their hidden messages. Man has come and gone through six millennia, but these two stone wonders stand as mute evidence of an Architect who understood the intricate workings of the universe, and the history and future of man on this planet. The story of the scarlet thread of redemption is woven into their geometry and their structure in ways that are too marvelous for our minds to fully comprehend.

The Great Pyramid is a magnificent structure. Its means of construction has baffled archaeologists and engineers, and although many theories have been presented through the years, yet no conclusive evidence has ever been presented to explain how the ancients lifted and placed its huge stones.

Those who have not seen the Great Pyramid can only imagine its enormity. Its base covers thirteen acres, and it contains enough masonry to build a sidewalk three inches thick and two feet wide that would reach around the world. It rises to a height comparable to a 40-story building that would fill seven blocks of midtown Manhattan. Those huge stones, some of which weighed as much as 50 tons, were cut to an accuracy of within 1/50 of an inch. The mortar between the stones was so thin it can scarcely be detected with the naked eyd, yet it was so strong that even after more than 4,000 years of the ravages of sun, rain, and the vandalism of man, the stones themselves will shatter before the mortar will yield.

In the year A.D. 820, the Caliph Al Mamoun, who was the ruler in Baghdad, heard a rumor that there were maps of the stars hidden in the Great Pyramid. Since he was an accomplished astronomer, the report was of much interest to him. He employed a vast number of architects, engineers and stone masons who set out for the Pyramid in the hopes of finding the long-hidden treasure.

The obvious gabled entrance that we see today had been carefully concealed by the white polished limestone casingstones that covered the entire Pyramid. Tradition held that the entrance was on the north face. For many days Al Mamoun and his workmen searched the north face for the mysterious hidden door, but with no success. So they decided to force their way through the solid limestone.

After tunneling more than 100 feet into the solid lime-

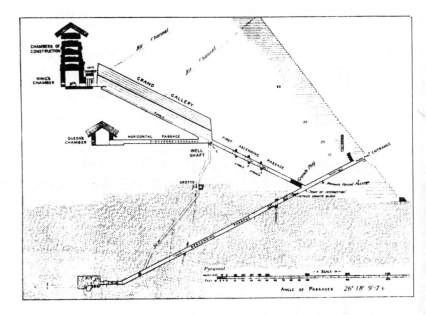

stone core, the men were becoming ill because the oxygen in the bore was being consumed by their flaming torches. Ready to accept defeat, their interest was suddenly renewed when they heard the muffled sound of something falling, just east of their bore. With renewed vigor they worked excitedly toward the direction of the sound.

They soon broke into a hollow passageway. On the floor before them lay a large angular stone that had been dislodged from the ceiling by the pounding of their hammers. They instinctively looked up. There above them was what seemed to be the beginning of a smoothly hewn passage, but it was completely filled with a huge red and black granite block.

Al Mamoun's magnificent discovery in A.D. 820

They realized that the angular stone that had fallen had been placed at the entrance of this passage by the builders, to conceal any evidence of an upper passage.

In all of Al Mamoun's studies of the Great Pyramid, he had found no mention of any upward passages. Realizing that the passage had been sealed and hidden since the time of the Pyramid's construction, he knew that he had made a great discovery.

The workmen attempted to break up the large granite stone that blocked the passage, but without success. So they decided to bore through the surrounding softer limestone. They found not one, but three huge granite plugs, completely filling the lower end of the ascending passage. After successfully boring beyond the granite, they emerged into the hidden passage – the first men to enter the passage since the completion of construction, more than 3,000 years previously.

Excitement was high! Perhaps now they could find the hidden treasures that the Pyramid was believed to hold.

Crawling on hands and knees, they soon reached the top of the narrow cramped passage. Before them was a marvelous sight – a large corbelled passageway, whose ceiling was so high it disappeared into the darkness above them.

Making their way with their torches, they found, at the top of the passage, a small narrow horizontal passage, again requiring them to resort to hands and knees. At the end of this very small passage, they emerged into a large room. The walls, floor and

The discovery of the upper passages and chambers.

ceiling were of beautifully polished red granite. At the far end of the room was a large granite box. Surely, they thought, this must contain the treasure.

In a fever of excitement, they rushed toward it. Their anticipation was at a peak. Their many weeks of agonizing labor was now to reap its reward.

But the men stopped, and silently looked with disbelief into the red granite box. It was completely empty. It contained no treasure, no celestial maps, no gold or jewels, and, most important of all, no mummy. They found it exactly as the builders had left it – open, empty and without a lid.

The Great Pyramid was, in fact, not a tomb at all. Evidence is definitely against the theory that grave robbers had previously removed the lid and the mummy. The only other opening that leads upward is the Well, and Al Mamoun found it completely filled with original construction debris, and totally impassable. In fact, it was not possible to climb the Well until the early 1800s, when it was finally cleared.

Even if it had been possible for the grave robbers to enter the upper chamber through the Well, they would not have been able to remove the lid or a mummy because the passages were simply too small to carry them through.

Since the granite box was also too large to fit through the passages, Al Mamoun reasoned that the chamber had been built *around* the box, and that the workmen then continued to build the upper portion of the Pyramid to its summit platform.

With the discovery of the upper passages and chambers, it became evident that no one had ever been buried in the Great Pyramid. Yet, the tomb theory persists. It has been suggested by many Egyptologists that it was the tomb of the Pharaoh Cheops. And that theory continues to be believed, even though the tomb of Cheops has been found in a separate grave nearby.

It is important to realize that the Great Pyramid has global, universal, scientific, and prophetic significance; and it is degrading to the importance and magesty of the structure to bring it down to the product of the pride of an ancient Pharaoh.

The prophet Isaiah spoke of this magnificent Pyramid, and said it would be for a *"sign and a witness"* in the last day. And, although he did not mention the Pyramid by name, his reference to it is unmistsakably accurate.

Isaiah wrote: *"In that day there shall be an altar to the Lord in the midst of the land of Egypt, and a pillar at the border thereof to the Lord. And it shall be for a sign, and for a witness unto the Lord of Hosts in the land of Egypt."* (Isaiah 19:19-20)

For nearly one hundred years, it has been known that the Gematria of that statement adds to 5449, and the height of the Great Pyramid, from its socket level base to its summit platform, is 5,449 Pyramid Inches. To be mathematically precise, it measures 5,448.96 Pyramid Inches. This accuracy of the Gematria could not have been the expertise of Isaiah, for it is not expected that he had access to the knowledge of the Pyramid's height. It more probably was the unfathomable knowledge of the One who gave the prophecy to Isaiah, for that One planted His signature there.

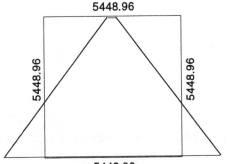

Perimeter of square: 21,795.84
21,795.84 ÷ 688 = 31.68
Jesus = 688
Lord Jesus Christ = 3168

The Apostle John said: *"All things were made by Him, and without Him was nothing made,"* (John 1:2) The very size of the earth is also shown in this remarkable height of the Great Pyramid, and it is connected to the name of Jesus. He left the unmistakable, indelible evidence, that this structure was a representation of His involvement with man and man's home, the earth. He knew that He would come to earth to redeem the race of Adam. He knew that His innocent blood would be the fulfillment of the scarlet thread. He planted it in the height of the Great Pyramid.

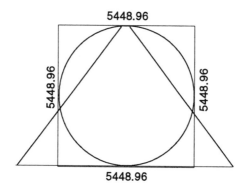

5448.96

5448.96

5448.96

5448.96

Circumference of circle: 17,118.398
17,118.398 ÷ 688 = 24.881392
Mean circumference of earth: 24,881.392 miles
Jesus = 688

The relationship of the height of the Great Pyramid to the circumference of the earth and to the name of Jesus is startling! The earth is the *place* of salvation, and He is the *means* of salvation. And the symbolism of the Great Pyramid is the salvation of man.

It also bears a remarkable relationship to earth's moon in its position at the head of the Nile Delta. Isaiah had said that this sign and witness would be in the midst of the land of Egypt and at the border thereof. There is only one spot on earth which answers to that description, and on that spot stands the Great Pyramid. It stands at the very center of the quadrant of the Nile Delta.

In 1868 the Chief Hydrographer for the United States Coastal Survey found that the extremities of the Nile Delta formed the quadrant of a circle, and he found that in the very center of that circle stands the Great Pyramid. With this discovery, he announced: "That monument stands in a more important physical situation than any other building erected by man." And indeed he was right!

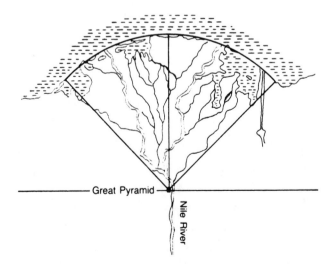

Let's go one step further. Let's draw the entire circle. We find that the distance from the center of the circle – the Great Pyramid – to the most northern tip of the Nile Delta, is 108 miles, making the diameter of the circle 216 miles. What a marvelous display of the knowledge of the Designer; for if we multiply those miles by ten, we have the diameter of the moon in miles.

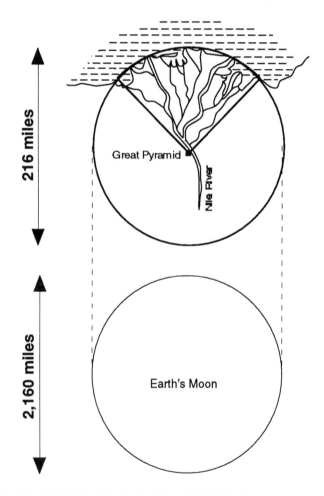

216 miles

Great Pyramid

Nile River

2,160 miles

Earth's Moon

The relationship of the Great Pyramid to earth and to earth's moon is magnificent! It gives evidence of having the same Architect. An Architect who knew the size relationship of earth and moon.

The moon is earth's only natural satellite. As the earth revolves around the sun every 365 whole days, its moon accompanies it on its celestial journey. They move as a unit. Therefore let's show the moon touching the earth, as the earth-moon unit. Think of the earth as a circle, even though in actuality it is flattened at the poles and bulges at the equator. The diameter of the circle becomes the equator. Draw connecting lines from both ends of the diameter up to the center point of the moon. It forms a triangle. But a very

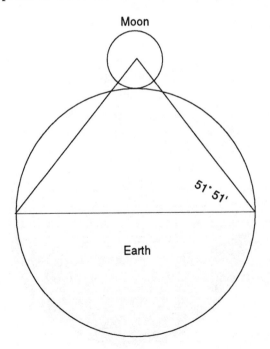

special triangle. It is, in fact, the precise proportions of the Great Pyramid, with a base angle of 51° 51', with its topstone sitting precisely in the center of the moon, just as the Great Pyramid sits at the very center of the circle of the Nile Delta. This identical geometry is not a product of blind chance – it bespeaks of plan and purpose.

Below is an illustration of this remarkable relationship of the Great Pyramid to the earth and its moon, drawn in three dimensions. The base perimeter of this earth-commensurate pyramid is 31,680 miles – bearing the name of its Maker, the Lord Jesus Christ, whose Gematria is 3168. The relationship of this square base to the earth, and to earth's orbit of the sun is the weaving of the scarlet thread

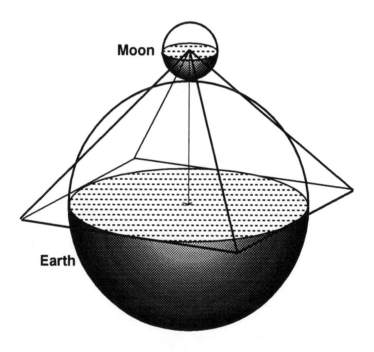

of redemption, placed into the base perimeter of the Great Pyramid, over 4,000 years ago.

Earth's orbit of the sun requires 365 whole days. And we have seen that the Gematria for "the scarlet" is 365. Also "scarlet" has a Gematria of 360, which denotes a circle. We are dealing with the circular orbit of the earth, rather than its elliptical orbit. However, the 365 whole days does not quite complete the circle. It actually requires 365.242 days.

The base perimeter of the original full design of the Great Pyramid, at its socket level has been precisely and accurately measured. The square base has been found to have a perimeter of 36524.2 Pyramid Inches. Remarkable! It appears to picture earth's orbit around the sun. Since the center of this square – if we were looking down on it from above – would be the topstone, we realize that this topstone would represent the sun. In the illustrations on the preceding pages, we have seen that the topstone sits at the center of the moon. The light from the moon is the reflected light from the sun.

We have seen in chapter 2 that the light from the sun which engulfs our earth bears the numbers of the Lord Jesus Christ and salvation. Now, we have the same illustration with the Great Pyramid. The topstone represents the light from the sun, and its base perimeter represents the orbit of earth around the sun. This base perimeter of the earth-commensurate pyramid measures 31,680 miles – the Gematria for Lord Jesus Christ, 3168. The base perimeter of the Great Pyramid is 36524.2 Pyramid Inches, relating to earth's orbit of the sun. Thus the Great Pyramid represents salvation through Jesus Christ. This relationship is shown in the illustration below. I have projected the base so it can be viewed in relation to the topstone at its center.

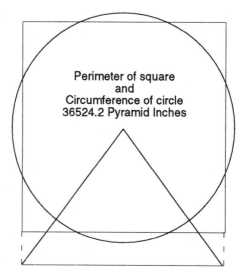

Perimeter of square
and
Circumference of circle
36524.2 Pyramid Inches

Although earth's orbit of the sun is an ellipse, the design of the Great Pyramid shows it as a square, which can be projected into a circle. It is evidence that the Word living, the Word written, the Word in number, the Word in stone, and the Word in the cosmos all tell the same story – the story of salvation. It is the story of the scarlet thread, the shedding of innocent blood to free the guilty. It is the story of the ages – the story of the innocent blood of Jesus Christ being shed for the guilty blood of Adam.

The Pyramid Inch is nearly identical to our British Inch. To convert a Pyramid Inch to a British Inch, simply divide the Pyramid Inch by .999. Thus 1,000 Pyramid Inches would equal 999 British Inches. The difference is practically negligible, however, to be precise, I have retained the Pyramid Inch as the unit of measure. Multiply the Pyramid Inch by 25 and we have a Pyramid Cubit.

The accuracy of these measures can be realized when we compute the base perimeter of the Great Pyramid. Measuring its original full design in Pyramid Cubits, we find that each side is precisely 365.242 units. What a design! It is the work of One who knew the orbit of the earth around the sun. Each side of its base measures 365.242 Pyramid Cubits, while its entire perimeter measures 36524.2 Pyramid Inches. Its message is shouting at us! It pictures earth's orbit around the sun.

Its message is that light from the sun is flooding and engulfing the earth as it makes its yearly trip. That light pictures Jesus, the *"Light of the World"* whose shed blood provides redemption from the Adamic curse. That precious innocent blood was pictured through the pages of the Bible as the scarlet thread of redemption. The Gematria for "scarlet" is 360, denoting a circle which has 360°. The Gematria for "the scarlet" is 365, telling us it is the circle of the orbit of the earth around the sun that is being pictured. Now we find this fully and beautifully illustrated in the relationship of the topstone of the Pyramid to its square base. Its message was an intended one. It was the design of a Great Designer, who planned for the salvation of man, long before man ever needed redemption.

Using the base perimeter of the original design of the Great Pyramid, we found that each side measures 365.242 Pyramid Cubits. However, the earth's orbit of the sun requires 365 whole days, with the .242 left over. Dealing with whole days the Gematria is astounding!

Using 365 as the measure for each side, let's draw a square representing the square base of the Great Pyramid. It will have a perimeter of 1460. Convert this to a circle having a circumference of 1460, then draw another square enclosing the circle. This new square will have a perimeter of 1860 units. Convert the 1860 into the circumference of a circle, and draw another square enclosing the new circle. This outer square will have a perimeter of 2368, which is the Gematria for Jesus Christ.

If this process is confusing, let me simplify it. First draw a square that represents the base of the Great Pyramid, with sides of 365 – "the scarlet" thread of redemption through the blood of Jesus Christ.

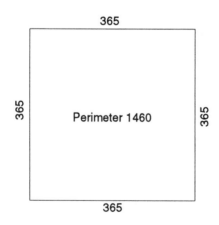

Next, convert the square to a circle with a circumference the same measure as the perimeter of the square.

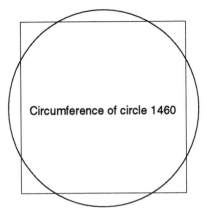

Circumference of circle 1460

Now draw a new square which will enclose the circle – in mathematics this is called superscribing a square on the circle.

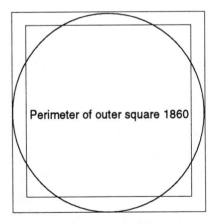

Perimeter of outer square 1860

The new (outer) square will have a perimeter of 1860. Repeat the process one more time, and the outer square will have a perimeter of 2368.

These four numbers, 365, 1460, 1860 and 2368 have remarkable significance in the Gematria of the Bible. They tell the story of redemption through Jesus Christ, and they were planted in the base perimeter of the Great Pyramid.

365 = The scarlet, חשני
1460 = A precious cornerstone, a sure foundation (Isaiah 28:6) Jesus is the cornerstone and the foundation.
186 = Golgotha, $\Gamma o\lambda\gamma o\theta\alpha.$ The place where the innocent blood was shed.
186 Relates to the speed of light. The light from the sun that engulfs earth.
2368 = Jesus Christ, $I\eta\sigma o\upsilon\varsigma\ X\rho\iota\sigma\tau o\varsigma$

It amazes me that the story of salvation – a process that has been working according to plan since before the creation of man – can be so beautifully told in such a short and concise statement as these 4 numbers portray. They tell of the innocent blood of Jesus Christ that would be shed on Golgotha's hill. They tell of the light that comes to us from the sun, flooding our earth with life and light. They tell of the life and light of Jesus Christ that will flood and engulf earth during the great Millennium. All this, in just four little numbers. God's word and His works are magnificent!

This is the story that has been hidden, written in stone, for more than 4,000 years, in what has come down to modern man as the world's greatest mystery – the Great Pyramid.

Just as the light from the sun, floods and engulfs our earth during every twenty four hours of its orbit around the sun, so the Great Pyramid is represented as receiving the light from its topstone, flooding and engulfing its entire mass, down to its very base. And, just as the earth is the place of salvation, so also is the Great Pyramid the story of salvation, written in stone.

Around the beginning of the 20th century, Bible scholars and pyramidologists began to uncover the meaning and purpose of the Great Pyramid, and to decipher its story of salvation. Today, its relationship to the salvation of man, is widely known.

Basic concept of salvation as shown in the Great Pyramid

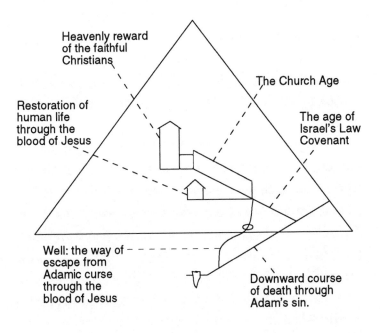

Heavenly reward of the faithful Christians

The Church Age

Restoration of human life through the blood of Jesus

The age of Israel's Law Covenant

Well: the way of escape from Adamic curse through the blood of Jesus

Downward course of death through Adam's sin.

THE GREAT PYRAMID AND STONEHENGE 113

The story is a simple one, yet, as with many apparently simple things, the more deeply we dig the more precious jewels of understanding we find. But its simple, apparent story of salvation is agreed upon by most – it is only the details upon which scholars differ.

The small chamber that represents the restoration of the earth and man upon it, is explained by some to represent the restoration of Israel. In reality the two concepts are one and the same. This small chamber has been named, in modern times, the Queen's chamber. This chamber has nothing to do with a queen, but that is the name that has

The Kingdom of Jesus Christ will rule from Jerusalem.

been given to it. Its geometry and its Gematria tell its story. It represents the kingdom of Jesus Christ, when He comes to take His place as the rightful ruler on the throne of David, setting up His righteous government in Jerusalem. And throughout the entire Millennium the blessings of life and peace and prosperity will flow from that government to all the farthest reaches of the earth.

The prophet Isaiah described the time when the blessings of life and peace will flow from Jerusalem to all the world. One such description is found in Isaiah 52:9-10: *"Break forth into joy, sing together, ye waste places of Jerusalem: for the Lord hath comforted his people, he hath redeemed Jerusalem. The Lord hath made bare his holy arm in the eyes of all nations; and all the ends of the earth shall see the salvation of our God."* This beautiful prophecy describes the rule of an iron hand in a velvet glove, and it ends by saying *"all the ends of the earth shall see the salvation of our God."* Yes, that Kingdom which He sets up in Jerusalem will, during earth's great Millennium, bring life and peace to all the *"ends of the earth."*

One of the beautiful features of this prophecy is the phrase *"the salvation of our God."* Its Hebrew letters add to 888, which is the number of the name Jesus. It is through Him that salvation comes to the whole race of Adam.

Again Isaiah gave us a prophetic picture of the blessings of life flowing from Jerusalem. This time he uses the picture of a mother nursing her children – the mother being Israel and the children the other nations of the earth.

The nations will be nourished as a suckling child.

"Rejoice ye with Jerusalem, and be glad with her, all ye that love her: rejoice for joy with her, all ye that mourn for her: That ye may suck, and be satisfied with the breasts of her consolations; that ye may milk out, and be delighted with the abundance of her glory. For thus saith the Lord, Behold I will extend peace to her like a river, and the glory of the Gentiles like a flowing stream; then shall ye suck, ye shall be borne upon her sides, and be dandled upon her knees. As one whom his mother comforteth, so will I comfort you; and ye shall be comforted in Jerusalem." (Isaiah 66:10-13)

Isaiah also described the time when all the other nations will desire to go up to Jerusalem to learn the ways of peace. *"And it shall come to pass in the last days, that the mountain* (Kingdom) *of the Lord's house shall be established in the top of the mountains* (above all other kingdoms), *and shall be exalted above the hills; and all nations shall flow unto it. And many people shall go and say, Come ye, and let us go up to the mountain of the Lord, to the house of the God of Jacob; and he will teach us of his ways, and we will walk in his paths: for out of Zion shall go forth the law, and the word of the Lord from Jerusalem. And he shall judge among the nations, and shall rebuke many people: and they shall beat their swords into plowshares, and their spears into pruninghooks: nation shall not lift up sword against nation, neither shall they learn war any more.*" (Isaiah 2:2-4)

It is describing a time when the nations of the earth will not even *"learn war."* They will not have a stockpile of nuclear weapons, and will not train soldiers to fight, but they will learn the ways of peace.

In Isaiah's description of this kingdom of peace, he said: *"for out of Zion shall go forth the law, and the word of the Lord from Jerusalem."* It was not by blind chance that the phrase *"the word of the Lord from Jerusalem"* adds to 864; the name Jerusalem (in Greek) adds to 864; and the perimeter of the Queen's Chamber is 864 Pyramid Inches. It was the design of the Architect, both of the Word written and the Word in stone.

864 = Jerusalalem, Ιερουσαλημ
864 = The word of the Lord from Jerusalem
864 Pyramid Inches, perimeter of
Queen's Chamber

Isaiah also told us that it will be a time when men will learn righteousness. Mankind has spent 6,000 years learning and practicing unrighteousness, making war, killing one another and polluting the earth – the very home that was given to them. But instead of a beautiful home, the earth has become a vast graveyard, attesting to the truth of the warning given to Adam and Eve, that if they sinned they would die. This downward course into eventual death is pictured by the descending passage in the Great

Through Adam's sin, the human race was plunged downward into death.

Pyramid. The only means of escape was the ascending passage. It represented the promises made to the nation of Israel that if they would obey, they would live. But the law that was given to them, which could have meant life if it had been obeyed, in reality brought death because they could not keep it. Thus the ascending passage was completely filled with an impassable and impenetrable granite plug – it represented the law given at Sinai.

There was one other means of finding the upper passages and chambers. It was through the well. It represents the only way of

The only way of escape was through the well – the shed blood of Jesus Christ.

escape from the downward course of the human race toward death – Jesus Christ. In reality, this well was filled with debris, and was impassable for over 3,000 years, but when cleaned out, it was found that it ascended to the very place where the death of Jesus is pictured on the Pyramid's time-line. Thus it beautifully pictures the working of the scarlet thread of redemption.

The upper end of the well brings us to the juncture of the horizontal passage leading to the Queen's Chamber, and the angular passage leading up to the King's Chamber. (Do not be misled by the names of these two chambers. They were named by those who knew not of its magnificent display of the plan of God for the salvation of man.) Thus it is through the precious, innocent blood of Jesus Christ, that a way was opened to life – either earthly or heavenly.

The horizontal passage leads to the Queen's Chamber, which, as we have seen, represents earth's Great Millennium, under the rulership of Jesus Christ, who sits on the throne of David. It fulfills the long promised Millennium, which is the 7th thousand years from the creation of Adam, and brings us to the beginning of the Great Eighth Day.

For many years I wondered why this Great Eighth Day – earth's New Beginning – was not pictured in the symbolism of the Great Pyramid. Then, in 1993, something astounding was discovered.

The Egyptian authorities realized that the interior of the Great Pyramid was being damaged by the breath, the sweat, and the hands and feet of thousands of tourists who had been allowed to climb its mysterious passages and chambers. Something must be done to preserve this most awesome artifact from our past. So they decided to investigate its ventilation system to see if it was still working, or if it was plugged with debris and bat dung. But inspecting these very small air channels was not a simple matter. They were only eight inches wide by eight inches high.

So a German team was called in, led by a robotics expert, Rudolf Gantenbrink, who developed a tiny robot, equipped with a video camera to explore the air channels, and send back pictures.

What they found could prove to be the greatest discovery of modern times. When they sent the robot up the south air channel from the Queen's Chamber, it stopped when it ran into a solid piece of rock that completely filled the channel. The pictures that it sent back revealed a stone door, a portcullis door, which could be opened only from the other side, by pulling it up. The pictures showed the two ends of a copper handle that would be on the other side of the stone slab. The discovery caused no small stir among pyramidologists.

What would be on the other side of the door? Would it be just a continuation of the air channel? Would it be a large room. Would the room contain a mummy? Would it contain the fortunes of a Pharaoh that had been successfully hidden from grave robbers for 4,000 years? Why was its only means of opening from the other side? Was it large enough for a human to enter, and if so, then how could anyone possibly enter it through a channel only eight inches by eight inches?

I found it significant that this newly discovered chamber is on the 75th course of masonry. The floor of the Queen's Chamber is on the 25th course of masonry, and the floor of the King's Chamber is on the 50th. Its relative position appears to be part of a pattern.

If this chamber (if that is what is behind the door) is reached by an extension from the Queen's Chamber, per-haps it represents that which fol-lows earth's Great Millennium, which would be earth's Great

The chamber of earth's Great Eighth Day

Eighth Day. Perhaps it could represent man in possession of all that had been lost through Adam's disobedience – perfection, and in relationship with their Creator as sons. This is what had been purchased for man by the precious blood of Jesus Christ – He bought back all that Adam had lost. It is the fulfilling of the completed story of the scarlet thread of redemption.

The tiny passage that leads to this newly discovered chamber is only 8 inches by 8 inches. Certainly not big enough for a human to pass through. However, the number 8 is full of significance in the Gematria of the Bible. It represents a new beginning through Christ Jesus. The fact that it is 8 inches by 8 inches, making such a small passage, well represents the completed work of the Kingdom of Jesus Christ, which brings man into the possession of all that Adam had lost through his disobedience. Adam had human perfection and an intimate relationship with his Creator as a son. That sonship will be restored to Adam's race by the end of the Millennium. It is the purpose and work of the Kingdom. And it can only be accomplished through the life-giving blood of Jesus Christ. Therefore the passage leading to the chamber of the Great Eighth Day bears the number 8. This new beginning is sometimes called God's Grand Octave. And entrance into it is through the One who bears the number 8 – Jesus, $I\eta\sigma\sigma\upsilon\varsigma$, 888.

The number 8 in the Gematria of the Bible attests to its meaning as the entrance into the New Beginning, the Great Eighth Day.

- 8 = Entry, באה
- 8 = Beginning, או
- 8 = Save, η
- 80 = To make perfect, כלל
- 88 = Victory, $\nu\iota\kappa\eta$
- 888 = Jesus, $I\eta\sigma\sigma\upsilon\varsigma$
- 888 = Salvation of our God, ישועת אלהינו
- 888 = I am the Life, $\varepsilon\iota\mu\iota\ \eta\ \zeta\omega\eta$
- 8 - The atomic number for Oxygen, the very breath of life.

John saw this New Beginning in vision. He said: *"And I saw a new heaven and a new earth ... And I heard a great voice out of heaven saying, Behold, the tabernacle of God is with men, and he will dwell with them, and they shall be his people, and God himself shall be with them, and be their God. And God shall wipe away all tears from their eyes; and there shall be no more death, neither sorrow, nor crying, neither shall there be any more pain: for the former things are passed away. And he that sat upon the throne said, Behold, I make all things new."* (Revelation 21:1-5)

This New Beginning is God's Grand Octave. Man has experienced the results of Adam's disobedience for 6,000 years. We are now on the threshold of the promised Kingdom of Jesus Christ, which is the 7th thousand-year epoch of time. It will be followed by the Great Eighth Day.

God's Work Week and the Grand Octave of Time

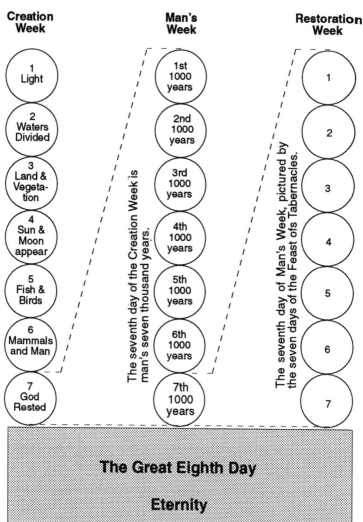

Creation Week

1 Light
2 Waters Divided
3 Land & Vegetation
4 Sun & Moon appear
5 Fish & Birds
6 Mammals and Man
7 God Rested

Man's Week

1st 1000 years
2nd 1000 years
3rd 1000 years
4th 1000 years
5th 1000 years
6th 1000 years
7th 1000 years

Restoration Week

1
2
3
4
5
6
7

The seventh day of the Creation Week is man's seven thousand years.

The seventh day of Man's Week, pictured by the seven days of Tabernacles.

The Great Eighth Day

Eternity

The seventh day of the Creation Week becomes the 7,000 years of man's period of fall, death, redemption and restoration. The seventh day of Man's Week becomes Earth's Great Millennium, which is divided into the seven days of the Feast of Tabernacles, which is followed by the Great Eighth Day.

This 7,000-year time-line of Man's Week begins with the date of the sin of Adam. It must be remembered that Adam was created near the end of the 6th Creation Day. The 7th day, in which God rested, began with Adam's sin. This 7,000-year span of Man's Week is woven into the geometry and design of the Great Pyramid.

By its passages and chambers, the Great Pyramid reveals the entire plan of God for the salvation of man, thus its symbolism covers the period from the time of Adam's sin, the time during which man is affected by that sin, and the time during which man is redeemed and restored to all that Adam lost. And, if the newly discovered chamber does indeed represent the Great Eighth Day, then it becomes apparent that the Great Pyramid also tells the story of man completely restored to all that Adam had before he sinned.

Students of the Pyramid (including myself) have attempted to find a time-line within its geometry and structure. Many theories have been put forth, most of which have been proven inaccurate by the passing of the dates predicted. However, there is a basic time-line that becomes evident in that it harmonizes with the Bible's description of 6,000 years of man's experiences, followed by earth's Great Millennium – a total period of 7,000 years.

On the following page is a scale drawing of the passages and chambers. This drawing was made long before the discovery of the possible new chamber by Rudolph Gantenbrink. It shows the south air channel from the Queen's Chamber reaching all the way to the outside. It is now known that it does not reach that far. However, if we follow the angle of the floor line of the ascending passages, projecting it both at the top and the bottom, its geometry suggests a time of 7,000 years (1 Pyramid Inch = 1 year).

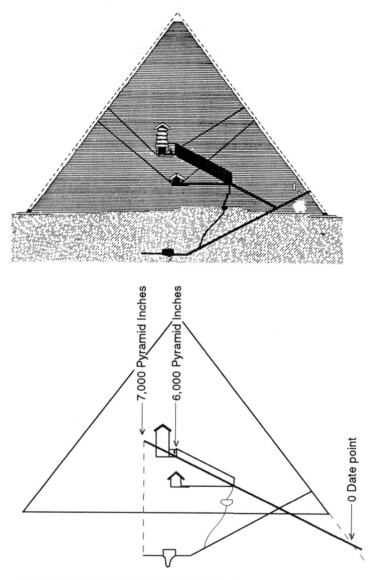

This book is not about chronology. However, the scarlet thread of redemption weaves its way through the time-line of the Great Pyramid in such a marvelous way, that I must include it in this work.

The pivotal points on this time-line are the birth and death of Jesus. This greatest event in the history of man – the life and ministry of Jesus – is shown as the focal point of all the passages. The date when the Lamb of God shed his innocent blood for the guilty blood of Adam becomes a fixed reference point on the time-line. Other dates and events are projected forward or backward from that pivotal point. It is a point on the floor of the Ascending Passage where the alignment of the north wall of the Grand Gallery intersects, and the alignment of the floor level of the Queen's Chamber intersects. All who see the Biblical symbolism in the Great Pyramid agree that this point of intersection sym-

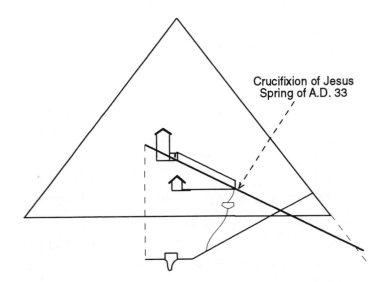

Crucifixion of Jesus
Spring of A.D. 33

THE GREAT PYRAMID AND STONEHENGE 125

bolizes the date of the crucifixion of Jesus. Even those who differ on that actual date in history, still agree that this special intersection marks the spot. Below is an enlargement of the area, showing the projected "Christ Triangle." This triangle accurately provides the relationship of His date of birth, baptism, and His death.

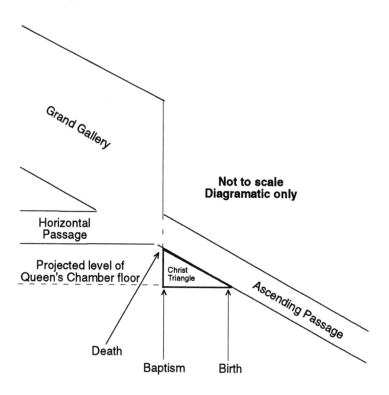

The construction of this right triangle is magnificent. And its placement at the top of the Ascending Passage tells us that it comes at the end of the age of the Law Covenant. Its juncture with the floor level of the Queen's Chamber tells us that it was His perfect human life that was offered in sacrifice; and its juncture with the beginning of the Grand Gallery tells us that through His life and death, He provided a new way for believers to walk – a new way of life – and eventually receive a heavenly reward. This grand upward way pictures the walk of the Christian.

Below is an enlargement of this right triangle, showing the preciseness of its portrayal of the life and death of Jesus. The measures are in Pyramid Inches, an inch for a year.

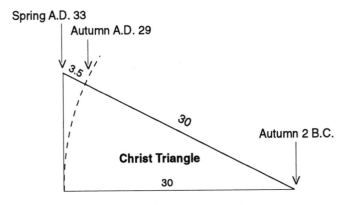

The Christ Triangle is at the top end of the Ascending Passage. The passage pictures the age of the Law, beginning with the Exodus, Passover, and the Law given on Mount Sinai, and ending with the birth and death of Jesus Christ – the antitypical Passover Lamb, and the One for whom the Law was to prepare Israel to receive. However, *"He came unto his own, and his own received him not."*

From the point which marks A.D. 33, at the top of the Ascending Passage, measuring down the floor of the passage to the point of intersection with the floor of the Descending Passage, is a length of 1543.5 Pyramid Inches[1]. However, counting the actual time back from the Crucifixion to the Passover, is 1480 years. The diagonal across the Descending Passage measures 60 Pyramid Inches[2], making the measure from the top to the intersection with the roof of the Descending passage 1483.5. If we repeat the Christ Triangle at this lower end of the Ascending Passage, it perfectly fits to the central axis of the Descending Passage, making the measure precisely 1480 Pyramid Inches, counting backward in time, from the Crucifixion back to the date of the Passover.

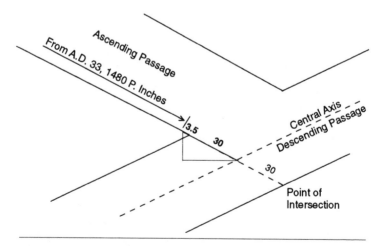

1 Morton Edgar, *The Great Pyramid: Its Scientific Features,* Bone & Hulley, Glasgow, 1924, p. 92

2 Morton Edgar, *The Great Pyramid: Its Spiritual Symbolism,* Bone & Hulley, Glasgow, 1924, p. 70

Are there any other indications that validate placing the time marker 3.5 inches into the passage? Yes! There are several.

First, measuring down the projected floor line of the Ascending Passage from this point, we find precisely 2520 Pyramid Inches to the zero point. It is not a random use of numbers. Many years prior to my observing this measurement, I had found in my studies in chronology that there are 2520 years between the sin of Adam and the first Passover. Now, seeing that it fits the projected floor line downward, I am thrilled

2520 years from Adam's sin to Israel's first Passover.

with the precision that it displays. It suggests that the Architect of the Great Pyramid knew history written in advance. This whole Ascending Passage, from its projected lower end to its top, pictures the story of the scarlet thread of redemption. Its lower terminal is at the zero date point, which is the time when Adam sinned, lost his justification, and his right to life. It was at that point in time that it became necessary that he have a redeemer if he would ever regain the life that had originally been given to him.

Moving up the projected floor line of the Ascending Passage 2520 inches (2520 years) brings us precisely to the year of the Exodus and the first Passover. The Israelites were instructed to kill a lamb and sprinkle its blood around the doorframes of their houses, that the firstborn of each household would be saved from death. It pictured the shedding of the blood of Jesus, the antitypical Passover Lamb.

Moving up the floor line of the passage 1480 inches

brings us to the Spring of A.D. 33, when Jesus hung on Calvary's cross, and His blood was spilled out upon the ground.

As shown previously, the number 1480 tells the story of the scarlet thread of redemption by Gematria.

148 = Blood
1480 = Tied on his hand scarlet
148 = Passover
1480 = Christ
1,480 years between typical and
antitypical Passover
1480 = Son of God
148 = Victory
1480 = His Kingdom

The years of man were obviously planned with precision, for the 2520 years from the sin of Adam to the first Passover is not just a random number. It is the Biblical number for "seven times" – 7 x 360 = 2520. How beautifully it tells the story of the scarlet thread, for the Gematria for "scarlet" is 360. This time span, from the sin of Adam to the Passover is, in fact, seven times scarlet. This 2520 years can be computed from the Biblical record. Basically it is:

1656 years from Adam's sin to the Flood
864 years from the Flood to the Exodus

2520 years from Adam's sin to the Exodus

2520 is the smallest number that is evenly divisible by all 9 digits.

This time span of 2520 years, followed by the 1480 years from the first Passover to the antitypical Passover, Jesus Christ, completes a span of 4,000 years.

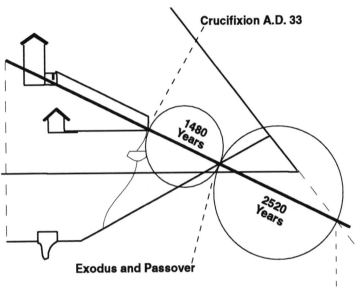

7 x Scarlet = 2520
Christ   = 1480
─────────
4000

A chronology of man, taken from the Bible and from other ancient records, reveals a time-span of 4,000 years from the sin of Adam to the year when the blood of Jesus was shed to redeem Adam and his race. The Bible's prophetic Word tells us there are 3,000 more years following the death of Jesus, fulfilling the whole span of 7,000 years of Man's Day, and bringing us to the New Beginning – the Great Eighth Day.

But what about the time between the creation of Adam and the day he sinned. Does that alter the Pyramid's timeline?

This is again revealed by the Christ Angle. This angle occurs at the top of the Ascending Passage, giving us the pivotal date point for the dating of the rest of the timeline.We moved it down to the juncture of the Ascending Passage and the Decending Passage to obtain the date of the Passover. Let's move it down again, to the bottom of the projected floor line, and find the years when Adam was sinless.

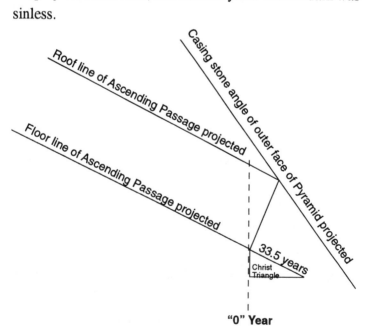

Is there any internal evidence in the Pyramid's time-line to warrant this suggestion? I believe there is.

Counting up the time-line 2520 years from minus 33.5 brings us to the central axis of the Descending Passage. Counting up from that point 480 years brings us to the year when David was anointed king over all Israel. David lived and reigned 33.5 years from that point.

Counting up the time-line from the year that David was anointed king over all Israel (1002 B.C.) exactly 1000 years, brings us to the date of the birth of Jesus, in the autumn of 2 B.C. Thus, from minus 33.5 to the birth of Jesus is 4,000 years. Jesus is the promised King who will sit on David's throne. Jesus is also the Second Adam. These two concepts are beautifully shown in the time-line.

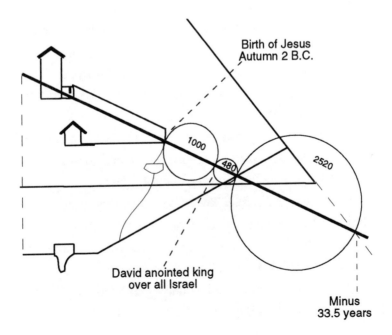

If Adam lived 33.5 years before he sinned, and if Jesus was the exact counterpart of Adam, taking his place in death, then it follows logically that Jesus would have lived as a perfect man for 33.5 years before He shed His blood for the blood of Adam.

The Pyramid's time-line appears to show these two 4,000-year time spans, offset by a brief period of 33.5 years.

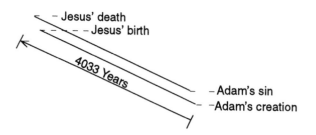

Upon first appearance, it might look as if the length of time should be 4033.5 rather than 4033. However, we are stating cardinal time, which says that the year is 4033, not ordinal time which says it is *during* the 4034th year.

This demonstration that the year 4033 from the creation of Adam is the year in which the Second Adam died, can be confirmed by another observation of the Great Pyramid. For this demonstration, let's look back at the illustration on page 103. It shows the Great Pyramid sitting at the exact center of a circle. The quadrant of that circle is the Nile Delta. Drawing a line connecting the farthest reaches of the delta forms a quadrant of a circle. It appears to be telling us that the Pyramid's relationship to the quadrant of a circle is important to understanding its secrets.

Let's draw a diagram of the Great Pyramid and the

quadrant of a circle, with the base of the casing stone angle placed at its center. And let's assign that quadrant a period of 7,000 years. The precise angle of the casing stones, from base to apex, will define a point of time on that 7,000 year time-line. When we do this, surprisingly we find that it will intersect the time-line at precisely 4033.

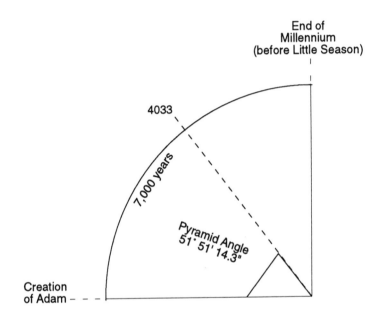

This demonstration is nothing short of magnificent! The math is exact. Archaeologists and Pyramidologists have carefully measured and calculated the outer angle of the Great Pyramid – its angle from base to apex. They have recorded it for us to the tenth of a second. This famous angle is 51° 51'14.3". When we convert to a decimal the figure is 51.8539722. Here is the math:

7000 years ÷ 90° = 77.777777 years per degree
77.777777 x 51.8539722 = 4033

Realizing the precision with which this calulation produces the year 4033, I wondered about something that I had written in a previous book, *Beginnings: the Sacred Design.* There I had illustrated the apparent use of the 7-pointed star in the design of the Great Pyramid. I had made the calculation graphically. It showed that the angles involved in the 7-pointed star were angles used in the construction of the Pyramid. Below is as it is shown in *Beginnings: the Sacred Design,* page 148.

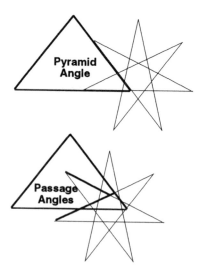

This shows that the angle from base to apex is the angle of a 7-pointed star; and the angle of the ascending and descending passages also fit a 7-pointed star. Graphically it appears to be exact, but mathematically it is not quite. While the true angle from base to apex is 51.8539722° the angle of a 7-pointed star is 51.428571 – a difference of .425401°. That is an acceptable difference to be considered the same, and so I used it in the illustration.

However, if we calculate it on the 7,000-year quadrant of a circle it produces the year of Jesus' birth. Here is the math:

7000 years ÷ 90° = 77.777777 years per degee
77.777777 x 51.428571 = 4000

Thus the difference between the Pyramid Angle and the angle of a 7-pointed star reveals a period of 33 years. Jesus was 33 when He was crucified on Calvary's cross.

Placing the Great Pyramid at the center of the circle is not just the musings of a mathematician. It actually and literally sits at the center of the circle that can be drawn on the Nile Delta. A circle is 360°, the same number as the Gematria for "scarlet." The symbolism tells us that that magnificent structure, holds the story of the scarlet thread of redemption. And indeed it does!

The very proportions of the structure bear the numbers of the place where Jesus hung on the cross, pouring out His innocent blood to redeem Adam. The measure of the base is the Golden Proportion of the measure of the two sides. Half the base is the Golden Proportion of one side. These proportions bear the number of Jesus Christ and the place where He died. And it sits in the center of a circle whose number is "scarlet."

On the following page is a diagram of the proportions of the Great Pyramid. I have assigned 186 units as the measure of its base. This will produce sides measuring 301. On page 58 is shown the "Golden Rectangle of His Passion, bearing the numbers 186 and 301. I will repeat it here.

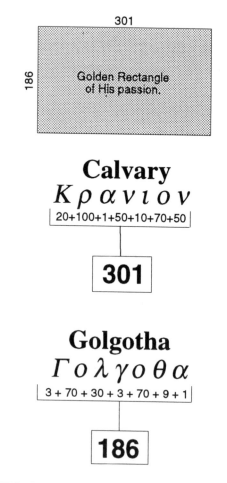

301

186

Golden Rectangle of His passion.

Calvary
Κ ρ α ν ι ο ν
| 20+100+1+50+10+70+50 |

301

Golgotha
Γ ο λ γ ο θ α
| 3 + 70 + 30 + 3 + 70 + 9 + 1 |

186

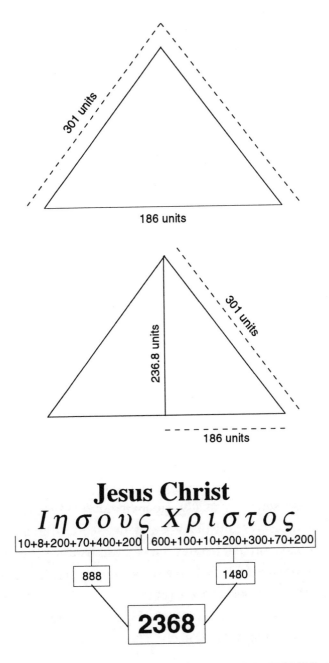

Jesus Christ

Ιησους Χριστος

| 10+8+200+70+400+200 | 600+100+10+200+300+70+200 |

888   1480

2368

THE GREAT PYRAMID AND STONEHENGE 139

No, the numbers are not just the musings of a mathematician – that is, not a human one. They bear evidence of being the plan of the Master Mathematician – the Creator – for they are also shown in the proportions of earth and its moon. And remember, the earth and its moon are a unit which orbits the sun. That orbit, when shown as a circle, has a diameter of 186 million miles.

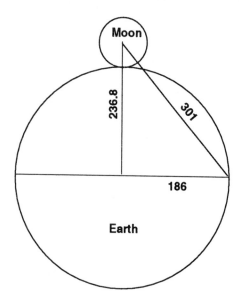

These are, of course, proportional measures. The actual measures are equally astounding. Just as the proportional measures tell the story of the scarlet thread of redemption through the shed blood of Jesus Christ, so the actual measures tell the same story. No wonder the Great Pyramid sits precisely at the center of the circle of the Nile Delta. And no wonder its angle of 51° 51' 14.3" gives us the very date of the crucifixion on Calvary.

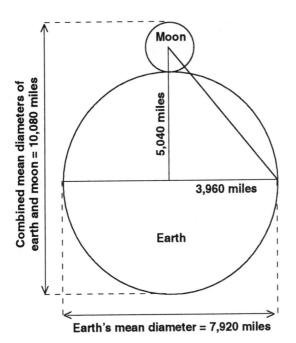

- **10080 =** He shall be great and shall be called the Son of the Highest, and the Lord God shall give Him the throne of David. (Luke 1:32)
- **792 =** Lord Jesus Christ (in Hebrew)
- **792 =** Salvation (in Hebrew)
- **396 =** Salvation (in Hebrew)
- **504 =** They pierced My hands and My feet (Psalm 22:16)
- **504 =** The house of David (Amos 9:11) (Prophetic of Jesus as the king on David's throne.)
- **5040 =** The kingdom of our Lord and His Christ (Rev. 11:15)
- **504 =** My salvation (Isaiah 56:10 (By multiplication)
- **504 =** Saviour (Isaiah 45:15) (By multiplication)
- **504 =** Christ (Greek) (By multiplication)

It's all about salvation through Jesus Christ! It is the central theme of the Bible. It is the story of the scarlet thread, telling of the promised redemption of man, and his complete restoration to all that Adam lost. That story is built into the geometry of our earth and moon. And it is built into the position of the Great Pyramid at the center of the quadrant of the Nile Delta. A realization of these facts tells us that it was an intentional design, and not just random chance. It tells us of the harmony of the Word written, the Word living, the Word in the cosmos, and the Word in stone.

The Word in stone has another witness, telling the same magnificent story. The prophet Jeremiah told us that God has *"set signs and wonders in the land of Egypt, and in Israel, and among other men."* (Jer. 32:20) And, indeed, there is a sign and wonder – a witness – *"among other men"* whose configuration is a circle, and bearing the same angle as the Great Pyramid. It is the monument that we now call Stonehenge.

Every summer, thousands of tourists come to Stonehenge to view the sunrise at the solstice. Watching

the sunrise at Stonehenge has become a tradition. In 1880 Professor William Flinders Petrie, commenting on such activities, wrote: "The large numbers of people that keep up with much energy the custom of seeing the sun rise at midsummer, somewhat suggests that it is an old tradition; and hence that it has some weight, independent of the mere coincidence."

That so-called "mere coincidence" produces numbers that are magnificent.

While standing in the center of Stonehenge, the summer solstice sunrise can be viewed in alignment with the Heel Stone, shown in the distance.

The Heel Stone has always been connected with the viewing of the summer sunrise. That remarkable stone was once called the Sunstone for this reason. In fact, the name Heel Stone comes from the Greek word for sun, *ηελιος, helios.*

From a position at the center of the Sarsen Circle, the sun can be viewed as it appears on the horizon, slightly to the left of the Heel Stone. Because it is at its most northern position, it rises at a sharp angle from the horizon. It appears momentarily to disappear behind the Heel Stone. Then in a burst of gold, it reappears as a crown of light atop the Heel Stone. And even though the sun slips back slightly along the ecliptic every year, yet in the 4,000+ years since Stonehenge was built, the sun has never left the Heel Stone at the solstice.

During those 4,000 years the precession of the sun along the ecliptic changes its position in relation to the Heel Stone. However, even after 4,000 years, the sun still crowns that stone with its golden glow. It has not separated from the Heel Stone. It will be more than 4,000 years into the future before it will be separated from that stone marker. Thus, even though the sun moves its relative position very slightly through time, the azimuth of sunrise at the summer solstice is marked by the permanent position of the Heel Stone.

A line drawn from the center of the Sarsen Circle to the center of the Heel Stone is 51° 51' from north. Exactly the same as the famous Pyramid angle. The positioning and building of Stonehenge, on the lonely island we now call

"British," was not the work of ignorant barbarians. It gives evidence of being part of a master plan, involving the redemption of man by the blood of Jesus Christ.

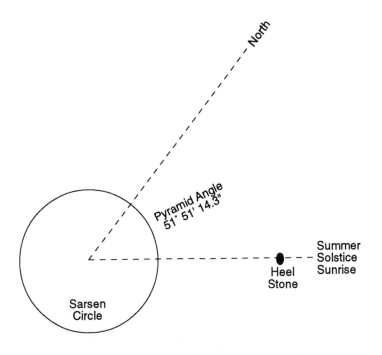

The quadrant of this circle, the same as the quadrant of the circle at the Nile Delta, represents the 7,000 years of man, from the fall to restoration. The angle of sunrise to north is precisely the same as the angle of the Great Pyramid, from base to apex. Thus measuring 51.8539722° from horizontal marks the year 4033 from the creation of Adam.

The location on which Stonehenge is built is the only place in the northern hemisphere where the angle of sunrise to north is precisely the same as the Pyramid Angle.

There is a corresponding location in the southern hemisphere, but it is on the ocean – thus this precise location in southern England is the only place on land where this stone witness could have been built.

This remarkable angle, drawn from the center of the Sarsen Circle, not only bears the number of the year 4033, it produces the same proportions as the Great Pyramid. Those proportions bear the numbers of Jesus Christ and the place of His death, Golgotha/Calvary.

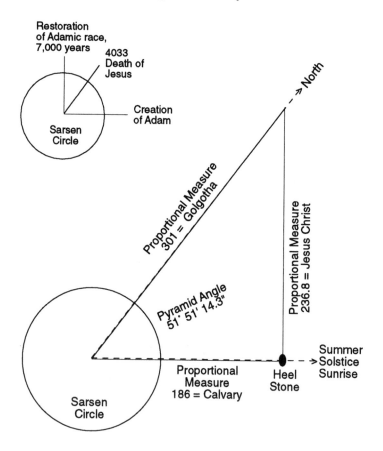

This evidence renders the Sarsen Circle at Stonehenge a most remarkable circle. And coupled with its circumference and its area, the evidence is overwhelming. That circle was designed by One who knew history written in advance. It is part of the Word in stone.

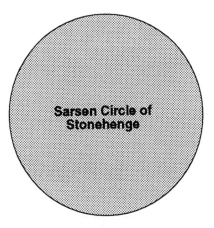

Circumference of Sarsen Circle = 316.8 feet
Lord Jesus Christ = 3168

Area of Sarsen Circle = 888 sq. yards
Jesus = 888

When we convert that circle into a square with the same perimeter, 316.8 feet, each side will measure 79.2 feet, or 26.4 yards. The numbers not only speak – they shout! They tell us that this circle represents Jesus Christ and His work of redemption for man. This remarkable circle, standing its lonely vigil on the Salisbury Plain in southern England for more than 4,000 years, is part of the weaving of the scarlet thread of redemption through the history of man.

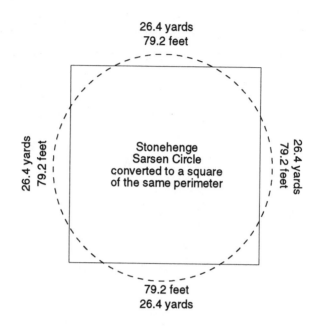

26.4 yards
79.2 feet

26.4 yards
79.2 feet

Stonehenge
Sarsen Circle
converted to a square
of the same perimeter

26.4 yards
79.2 feet

79.2 feet
26.4 yards

316.8 feet = **perimeter of square**
79.2 feet = **each side of square**
26.4 yards = **each side of square**
105.6 yards = **perimeter of square**

3168 = Lord Jesus Christ, *Κυριος Ιησους Χριστος*
792 = Lord Jesus Christ, אלהא יהושע משיח
264 = The Truth, *η αληθης*
1056 = The joy of Thy salvation, ששון ישעך

6

Scarlet:
the Color of Salvation

Hymn book theology tells us that we can be washed in the blood of Jesus Christ and be made white. The concept is not as contrary to nature as it may first appear.

As a child, I used to wonder how you could wash something in blood and make it white. Blood stains. And even removing a spot of blood from a white garment can only be done with the utmost care and expertise, else the stain will remain. Yet, Isaiah said, *"Come now, let us reason together, saith the Lord: though your sins be as scarlet, they shall be as white as snow; though they be red like crimson, they shall be as wool."* (Isaiah 1:18)

Isaiah did not really spell it out regarding the *method* of making them white as snow, he only said they would be. The Apostle John alluded to it when he said *"The blood of Jesus Christ ... cleanseth us from all sin."* Then, in his Revelation that he received as an old man, he dedicated his writing *"Unto Him that loved us, and washed us from our sins in His own blood."* (Revelation 1:5) Then it was spelled out in no unmistakable terms in Revelation 7:14: *"These are they which came out of great tribulation, and have washed their robes, and made them white in the blood of the Lamb."*

Isaiah had told us that the sins are scarlet, and John

told us that those sins are removed by the blood of Jesus Christ. The obvious analogy is that we are removing red by using red – removing red sins by using red blood. But how does this process make anything white?

The answer came forcefully to me one day many years ago. Before I retired, I worked as a graphic designer for a printing firm. Often in the course of my work, it was necessary for me to go into the darkroom. A darkroom is exactly that – all the lights are out, and it is completely dark, except for one thing. In order for the worker to see, the room is equipped with red lights. Photographic film sees red as if it were black, and thus the red lights will not expose the film. There is no other light in the room than red light.

One day I was wearing a white shirt with large red spots on it. That day it was necessary for me to do some work in the darkroom. As I entered the room and closed the door behind me, I suddenly noticed that all the red spots on my shirt had disappeared, and the shirt was completely white. I was the only person in the darkroom, and I stood there with tears of joy running down my face, for I suddenly realized the true meaning of being washed in the blood of Jesus. My sins were like those big red spots on my white shirt. And the red light in the room was like the blood of Jesus, which totally and completely cancelled out the spots and made my shirt white.

My sins – those big red spots on my shirt – were because of the sin of Adam, and I am a descendant of Adam and therefore have inherited a sinful nature. But the blood of Jesus – those red lights – took all my spots away, and left me white. I realized that this was the true meaning of the comparison that the Apostle Paul was making in the fifth chapter of Romans.

"Wherefore, as by one man sin entered into the world, and death by sin; and so death passed upon all men, for that all have sinned ... if through the offence of one, many be dead, much more by the grace of God, and the gift by grace, which is by one man, Jesus Christ, hath abounded unto many ... for if by one man's offence death reigned by one; much more they which receive abundance of grace and of the gift of righteousness shall reign in life by one, Jesus Christ. Therefore as by the offence of one, judgment came upon all men to condemnation; even so by the righteousness of one, the free gift came upon all men unto justification of life."

Scarlet: the color of sin. Scarlet: the color of salvation.

Adam and his race have been washed in the blood of Jesus Christ, and will come out white.

Scarlet is the color of sin, and scarlet is the color of salvation.

The scarlet thread of redemption began weaving its way through the pages of time from the foundation of the world. When Adam sinned, God killed an innocent animal, shedding its innocent blood, that He might clothe Adam with its skin, symbolically covering Adam by means of the blood of Jesus. The period during which this is fully enacted in the experience of man is 7,000 years – the span of time from the sin of Adam to the complete restoration of Adam and his race. A restoration to all that Adam had lost. The story of the scarlet thread covers a period of 7,000 years. The key Figure in this transaction is the Lord Jesus Christ, for it was His substitutionary blood that paid the price for sin. He was the *"Lamb slain from the foundation of the world,"* (Revelation 13:8).

In chapter 2 we saw the remarkable use of the number 74 in the Gematria of the Bible. It is a foundation number. We saw that both 12 and 74 were foundation numbers; and 12 times 74 equals 888, which is the number for Jesus. Now let's look at some remarkable additions to that foundation principle. It is all tied together with the scarlet thread – the blood of Jesus Christ. It began from the foundation of the world, and will see the completion of its work by the end of 7,000 years.

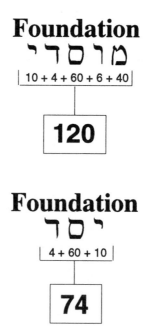

Foundation

מ ו ס ד י

| 10 + 4 + 60 + 6 + 40 |

120

Foundation

י ס ד

| 4 + 60 + 10 |

74

12 x 74 = 888

Jesus

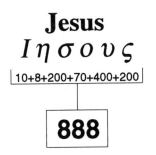

$I \eta \sigma o \upsilon \varsigma$

10+8+200+70+400+200

888

Creation

$\kappa \tau \iota \sigma \iota \varsigma$

20+300+10+200+10+200

740

You have laid the foundation of the earth

הארין יסדת

400 + 4 + 60 +10 + 50 + 10 + 200 + 1 + 5

740

Blood of Jesus

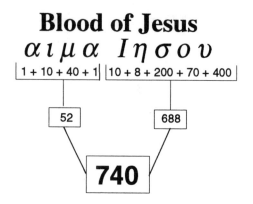

$$\alpha \iota \mu \alpha \quad I \eta \sigma o \upsilon$$

| 1 + 10 + 40 + 1 | 10 + 8 + 200 + 70 + 400 |

52   **688**

740

The Redeemer

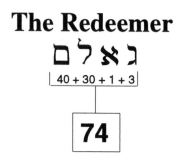

גאלם

| 40 + 30 + 1 + 3 |

74

Circle

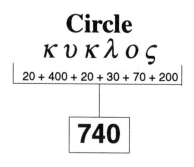

$$\kappa \upsilon \kappa \lambda o \varsigma$$

| 20 + 400 + 20 + 30 + 70 + 200 |

740

Circular

סביב

| 2 + 10 + 2 + 60 |

74

The Gematria is overwhelming! The number 74 pertains to creation, the foundation of the earth, Jesus as the Redeemer, His blood as the price of redemption, and to a circle. Why is the circle added to this list? Because a circle has 360°, and the word "scarlet" has a Gematria of 360. To trace around a circle, we always come back to the point at which we started. The scarlet thread of redemption tells the story of the creation of Adam in perfection, his fall from that perfection, the redemption of his life by the shedding of innocent blood on his behalf, and his restoration to all that he had lost. It comes full circle, back to the condition he had before he sinned. The process covers a span of 7,000 years.

The circle is an illustration of the story of redemption, salvation, and restoration.

Jeremiah told us that God had set signs and wonders in the land of Egypt (the Great Pyramid), and in Israel, and among other men (Stonehenge is probably one of them). I suggest that the sign and wonder in Israel was Solomon's Temple. It was a magnificent structure.

Immediately outside the Temple, in the courtyard, was

a large receptacle for water. It was called the Molten Sea. It was circular, and was supported on the backs of 12 oxen, cast in copper. The geometry of its design is marvelous.

"Also he made a molten sea of ten cubits from brim to brim, round in compass, and five cubits the height thereof; and a line of thirty cubits did compass it round about ... It stood upon twelve oxen, three looking toward the north, and three looking toward the west, and three looking toward the south, and three looking toward the east: and the sea was set above them, and all their hinder parts were inward. And the thickness of it was a handbreadth, and the brim of it like the work of the brim of a cup, with flowers of lilies; and it received and held three thousand baths." (II Chronicles 4:2-4)

Using the temple cubit, this would render the diameter of the Molten Sea 198 inches, or 16.5 feet. It was indeed a massive basin. No wonder it was called a *"sea."* Its function was for the purpose of washing.

Looking down on the Molten Sea it would appear as a circle, with the heads and shoulders of the twelve oxen pointing in the four cardinal directions.

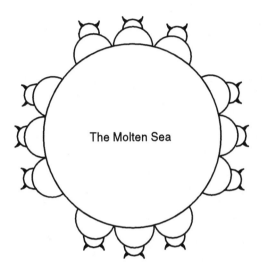

The Molten Sea

The design, construction and placement of this Molten Sea continues the story of the scarlet thread. This Sea was placed outside the Temple, which was built on the same hill where Abraham offered Isaac. Remember, though, that Isaac was not really killed, for God provided a ram in his stead. Both Isaac and the ram pictured the offering of Jesus upon that same hill. Today, the temple mount and the place of Golgotha are separated by excavations for building purposes. It was originally all one hill. This hill was a very special place. It was the meeting place between God and man. It was the place where the blood of redemption was poured out upon the ground, providing salvation for Adam and his race.

The circle of the Molten Sea bears the number of salvation. It is not by blind chance that its diameter measured ten cubits. If we were to superscribe a square on that circle, it would have a perimeter of 792 inches.

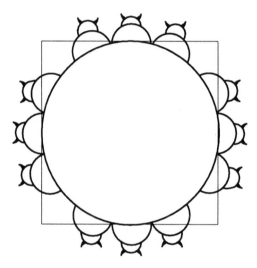

792 inches = perimeter of square
792 = Salvation, ישועות
792 = Lord Jesus Christ, אלהא יהושוע משיח

The purpose of the Molten Sea was for washing. Its numbers tell us that it represents salvation through Jesus Christ. The Apostle Paul talked of this washing. He called it *"the washing of water by the word,"* (Ephesians 5:26).

The only place in all of God's universe where salvation is needed and supplied is our planet earth. Thus the earth has a diameter of 7,920 miles – the number of salvation. Throughout the history of man on this earth, we find the weaving of the scarlet thread of redemption. Yes, the color of salvation is indeed scarlet.

The number of salvation has been shown in the size and relationship of the earth and its moon. It has been shown in the Great Pyramid, and in Stonehenge. And now we have seen that it was also shown in the Molten Sea which was placed in front of Solomon's Temple. The design of all of these falls into a pattern, both graphically and numerically. They obviously all have the same Architect.

Let's view these patterns as they relate to each other and observe the marvelous design of the Architect. We'll begin with the earth-moon unit. The illustration below shows a square drawn on the diameter of the earth. The square has a perimeter of 31,680 miles, which corresponds to the Gematria for Lord Jesus Christ, which is 3168. It shows the apex of a pyramid reaching to the center of the moon. If we were to draw a circle surrounding the earth which passes through this center point of the moon, its circumference would be 31,680 miles (using 22/7 for π). This places the circle of the earth and the circle through the center of the moon in the precise relationship as the Bluestone Circle has to the Sarsen Circle at Stonehenge.

Note the similarity of the design in each of the patterns below. It gives evidence of a Master Designer.

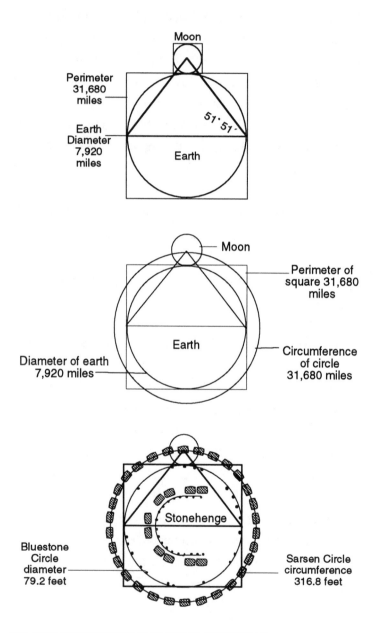

Moon

Perimeter
31,680
miles

Earth
Diameter
7,920
miles

Earth

51° 51'

Moon

Perimeter of
square 31,680
miles

Earth

Diameter of earth
7,920 miles

Circumference
of circle
31,680 miles

Stonehenge

Bluestone
Circle
diameter
79.2 feet

Sarsen Circle
circumference
316.8 feet

160 THE STONES AND THE SCARLET THREAD

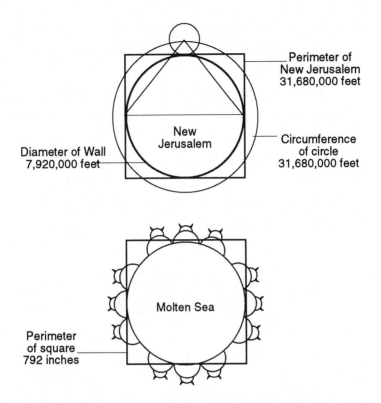

Perimeter of
New Jerusalem
31,680,000 feet

New
Jerusalem

Circumference
of circle
31,680,000 feet

Diameter of Wall
7,920,000 feet

Molten Sea

Perimeter
of square
792 inches

The pattern, the numbers and the Gematria tell us that an intentional design was involved. It also tells us that the same Architect originated the plan for each. It was an Architect who also designed the plan for the salvation of man.

Upon first glance, we might wonder if the dimensions given for the Molten Sea are contrary to the laws of mathematics, for the record gives the diameter of the Sea as ten cubits, and the circumference as thirty cubits. Mathematically this is not possible. However, if we take into consideration the thickness of the basin, and realize that the measure of the diameter is an outside measure, and the measure of the circumference is its mean, it becomes apparent that there is no problem.

It is entirely possible that these two measures – ten cubits and thirty cubits – were used in the text because their Gematria suggests a relationship of the Molten Sea with the salvation of man through the blood of Jesus Christ. We have already seen that a square drawn on the diameter of ten cubits will produce a perimeter of 792 inches, and the number for salvation is 792.

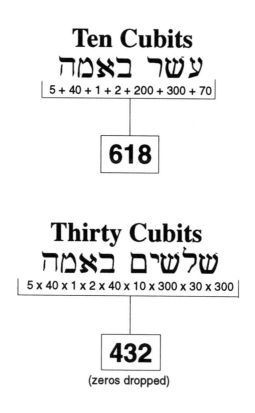

Ten Cubits

עשר באמה

5 + 40 + 1 + 2 + 200 + 300 + 70

618

Thirty Cubits

שלשים באמה

5 x 40 x 1 x 2 x 40 x 10 x 300 x 30 x 300

432

(zeros dropped)

On pages 51 through 53 we saw the remarkable use of the number 432 in the Gematria of the Bible. It pertains to man and to salvation. The number 432 tells us that salvation will include the entire world, the whole habitation of man; and it tell us the means of this salvation – the Lord Jesus Christ.

432 = Habitation

432 = World

432 = All things

432 = All nations

432 = Saviour

432 = The Branch of Jehovah

432 = Bethlehem

432 = Gethsemane

432 = Jerusalem

432 = Last Adam

The story told by the number 432 is the same story that is told by the circumference of the Molten Sea. The waters it contains are for washing – the washing away of Adamic sin by the blood of Jesus Christ, the Last Adam. The square drawn around this circumference bears the number 792, which is the Gematria for salvation and for Lord Jesus Christ. Surely the One who designed the Molten Sea and its dimensions was placing there the promise of the scarlet thread of redemption.

Isaiah had told us, *"Though your sins be as scarlet, they shall be as white as snow; though they be red like crimson, they shall be as wool."* The Gematria tells us that the effect of washing in the blood of Jesus Christ will be worldwide.

They shall be as wool

כ צ מ ר י ה י ו

6 x 10 x 5 x 10 x 200 x 40 x 90 x 20

432

(zeros dropped)

The ten cubits of the diameter of the Molten Sea has a Gematria of 618. It is the number of the Golden Proportion, which is 1:1.618, or shortened to .618. It is another example of a circle being used to show the Golden Proportion. The use of this number also points to Jesus Christ as the means of salvation. We have seen that the place where His innocent blood was shed for Adam – Calvary and Golgotha – bears the numbers 301 and 186. The number 186 is the Golden Proportion of 301 This can be shown either as a Golden Rectangle or as the proportions of the Great Pyramid.

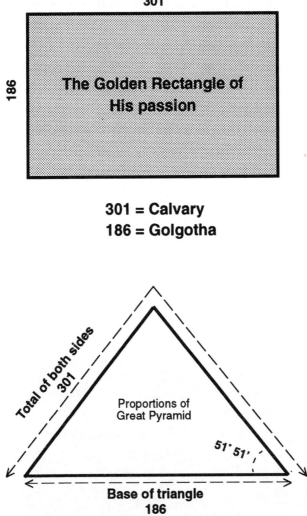

301 = Calvary
186 = Golgotha

The Golden Proportion not only shows the place of His death, it also shows the place of His birth – Bethlehem. The prophet Micah spoke of this when he wrote: *"But thou, Bethlehem Ephratah, though thou be little among the thou-*

sands of Judah, yet out of thee shall he come forth unto me that is to be ruler in Israel; whose goings forth have been from of old, from everlasting." (Micah 5:2)

Translating this exactly as the words appear in the Masoretic Text, this verse begins by saying, *"And you, Bethlehem Ephratah, least."* Its Hebrew letters add to 1958. I was astonished to find the same number used when Matthew quoted this prophecy. Using the Greek Nestle Text it reads, *"You, Bethlehem in Judea."* Its Greek letters add to 1958. The number 1958 is the Golden Proportion of 3168, the number for Lord Jesus Christ. It was no mistake. It was no mere chance happening. It was part of a divine pattern.

The place of Jesus' birth was prophesied – it was Bethlehem the Beautiful (Ephratah).

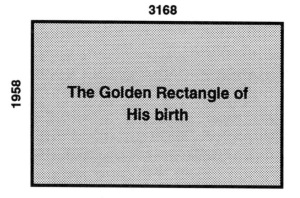

3168

1958

The Golden Rectangle of His birth

3168 x .618 = 1958

3168 = Lord Jesus Christ,
Κυριος Ιησους Χριστος

1958 = And you, Bethlehem Ephratah, least,
ואתה בית-לחם אפרתה צעיר

1958 = You, Bethlehem in Judea,
συ εν Βηθλεεμ της Ιουδαιας

This relationship of the Golden Proportion to the place of His birth can also be shown in the proportions of the Great Pyramid.

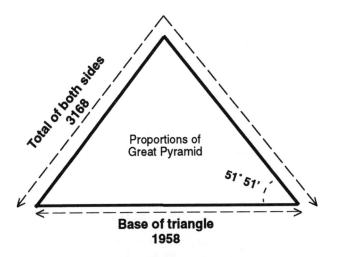

When Isaiah told us *"Though your sins be as scarlet, they shall be as white as snow; though they be red like crimson, they shall be as wool,"* he probably did not realize that the words he was penning held the secrets of the weaving of the scarlet thread by its Gematria. His hand was apparently being guided by a greater Hand. For the number values of *"they shall be as wool,"* when multiplied, produce 432. The place where that redeeming blood was poured out upon the ground was just outside the city of Jerusalem. It bears the number 432.

432 = They shall be as wool (by multiplication)
432 = Jerusalem (by multiplication)

Isaiah's use of the term "as scarlet" multiplies to 120. And, as we have seen, the word "scarlet" adds to 360. It does not go unnoticed that 120 x 360 = 432 (dropping the zeros).

When God gave the instructions for the building of the Temple and the Molten Sea, He described the Sea as being circular and measuring *"thirty cubits."* Those Hebrew letters multiply to 432. But the word *"circling"* adds to 120.

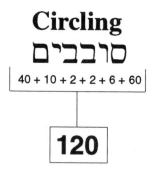

Circling
סובבים
40 + 10 + 2 + 2 + 6 + 60

120

Scarlet

שָׁנִי

| 10 + 50 + 300 |

360

The number 360 denotes a circle, for there are 360° in a circle. It is a fitting symbol because the complete work of the scarlet thread brings man full circle, back to all that Adam had before he sinned. This is the meaning and purpose of redemption. It is God's grand circle of time, that brings man to the threshold of His great Eighth Day. It brings man's place of habitation, the earth, back into harmony with their Creator. It is characterized by the number 432.

360 = Scarlet
120 = Circling

120 x 360 = 432

432 = Habitation
432 = World
432 = All things
432 = All nations
432 = Saviour
432 = Bethlehem
432 = Gethsemane
432 = Jerusalem
432 = Last Adam

The numbers tell the story so beautifully it leaves me standing in awe.

The story of the scarlet thread was mentioned by Solomon in one of his "songs."

There is debate among scholars regarding the purpose and interpretation of the Song of Solomon. It is obviously a love song. Some feel it is an allegory of the love relationship between Christ and the church, and/or the relationship between God and Israel. Some also feel it has apocalyptic overtones.

In Song of Solomon 4:3 the Lover tells the beloved, *"Thy lips are like a thread of scarlet."* In verse 4 He tells her, *"Until the day break, and the shadows flee away ... "*

The Gematria reveals the song to be prophetic – yes, even apocalyptic. *"A thread of scarlet"* has a numeric value of 388. Other uses of 388 reveal its meaning. It tells of the time when Shiloh (Jesus) comes to take His rightful place on the throne of David – the time of the sounding of the trumpet for the "catching away" of the bride.

388 = Scarlet Thread
3880 = The throne of His father David
388 = Shiloh
388 = To sound a trumpet

That time is at the ending of man's 6,000 years and the beginning of the seventh thousand. Today we stand on the threshold of the dawning of that new thousand-year "day." And so He tells His beloved, *"Until the day break, and the shadows flee away."* The Hebrew letters in this promise have a total numeric value of 792, the number of salvation.

> **7,920 miles - diameter of earth, the *place* of salvation**
> **792 = Salvation**
> **792 = Until the day break and the shadows flee away**
> **792 = His going forth is established as the dawn** (Hosea 6:3)

In Hosea 6:3 the salvation of Israel is said to be *"after two days"* and *"on the third day."* The third day from the coming of their Messiah (even though they did not recognize Him as such) is the great seventh day of man's 7,000-year span – the dawning of Earth's Great Millennium.

There were a few, though, in Israel who recognized Him as their long-promised Messiah. When Jesus was eight days old, his parents brought him to the Temple to present Him to the Lord. There was a man named Simeon who was led of the Holy Spirit to enter the Temple at that time. Simeon was a devout man, and he longed for and waited for the *"consolation of Israel."* He had been told that he would not see death until he had seen the Messiah. When he saw the baby Jesus he took the child in his arms and said, *"Lord, now lettest thou thy servant depart in peace, according to thy word: for mine eyes have seen thy salvation, which thou hast prepared before the face of all people; a light to lighten the Gentiles, and the glory of thy people Israel."* (Luke 2:29-32.)

Simeon apparently knew Isaiah's prophecy of the coming of the Messiah: *"Break forth into joy, sing together, ye waste places of Jerusalem: for the Lord hath comforted his people, he hath redeemed Jerusalem. The Lord hath made bare his holy arm in the eyes of all the nations; and all the ends of the earth shall see the salvation of our God."* (Isaiah 52:9-10)

Isaiah's phrase *"the salvation of our God,"* has a number value of 888. Picture Simeon standing there in the Temple, holding in his arms this very special child, and saying to all who were there, *"Mine eyes have seen thy salvation."* He was quoting Isaiah's prophecy. He held within his arms the child whose number is 888.

888 = The salvation of our God
888 = Jesus

Thirty three and one half years later, He hung upon a cross on Calvary's hill, pouring out His life blood for the sin of Adam – the fulfillment of the scarlet thread. He was the One Isaiah had prophesied would be led to the slaughter.

888 = "As a lamb to the slaughter he was led and as a ewe before her shearers." (Isaiah 53:7)

7

Water from the Rock

We all know that water does not flow from a rock. That is, not ordinarily. Water may flow through a channel in the rock, but such water usually comes from a spring or an underground stream. A small rock, that can be carried on the shoulders of men cannot produce water.

Yet, we have the testimony of many of the Old Testament writers that water indeed did flow from a very special rock. The story begins with Moses and the Israelites during their wilderness journey, after leaving Egypt. The people were thirsting in the desert of Sinai. God instructed Moses to strike a rock to get water. Moses probably had mixed emotions about this. In the first place, he might have been embarrassed to do such a thing in front of the people; but, secondly, he was a man of great faith, and had been given ample evidence that God was guiding him. After all, God had miraculously given him power to smite the Nile river and its waters turned to blood. So Moses was not proceeding on blind faith when he followed the instructions, and smote the rock. The waters gushed out!

The first mention of obtaining water from the rock may give the appearance that it was a rock native to the area, and perhaps permanently a part of the terrain. However, many years later, Moses was again told to obtain water from the rock, and in this account of the incident, it becomes apparent that the rock was familiar to them.

"And the Lord spake unto Moses, saying: Take the rod, and gather the assembly together, and speak ye unto the rock before their eyes; and it shall give forth his water, and thou shall bring forth to them water out of the rock.... And Moses and Aaron gathered the congregation together before the rock..., and Moses lifted up his hand, and with his rod he smote the rock twice; and the water came out abundantly, and the congregation drank and their beasts also." (Numbers 20:5-11)

It must be realized that the Israelites had moved no less than twenty-one times since the first incident of obtaining water from the rock, and were now in a location in a far different part of the desert.

They carried the rock with them on their wilderness journey.

Yet Moses was told to *"gather the congregation together before the rock."* What rock? They did not need to be told what rock – they knew. It was a rock they carried with them.

The Apostle Paul settled the matter regarding the portableness of the rock. He said, *"And all did drink the same spiritual drink; for they drank of that spiritual Rock that followed them: and that Rock was Christ."*

The word *"followed"* is from the Greek ακολουθεω, which literally means to carry along with or to accompany.

Paul not only settled the matter that the rock was portable, and went with them, he also informed us of its symbolism – it represented Christ. Why? Because it was the means of salvation to the Isrealites while in the desert. It literally saved them from dying of thirst. Thus it follows logically that the Gematria for *"water out of the rock"* is 426, and the Gematria for *"Saviour"* is 426.

426 = Water out of the rock, מים מצור
426 = Saviour, מושיע

It may be difficult for us today to picture water coming out of such a small rock, especially the quantity that would be needed to quench the thirst of more than two million people plus their cattle and other livestock. However, when this event was recalled by King David more than 500 years later, he spoke of water enough to fill a river.

"He brought streams also out of the rock, and caused waters to run down like rivers," (Psalm 78:16).

"Behold he smote the rock, that the waters gushed out, and the streams overflowed," (Psalm 78:20)

"He opened the rock, and the waters gushed out; they ran in the dry places like a river," (Psalm 105:41).

About 500 more years after King David's time, the prophet Isaiah spoke of the same event. The Gematria of Isaiah's words tell us that the event pictured salvation. Yes, just like the water that was in the Molten Sea pictured the blood of Christ, so the water that came from the rock which they carried with them through the wilderness was part of the thread of scarlet which is woven through the history of man. The rock pictured Jesus, the *"rock of our salvation."* And the water flowing from it pictured His blood which flowed out upon the ground as he hung upon the cross of Calvary.

Isaiah's words were: *"And they thirsted not when he led them through the deserts: he caused the waters to flow out of the rocks for them: he clave the rock also, and the waters gushed out,"* (Isaiah 48:21) Reading this, exactly as it appears in the Masoretic Text, it says, *"And not they thirsted in the deserts."* The Hebrew words add to 792.

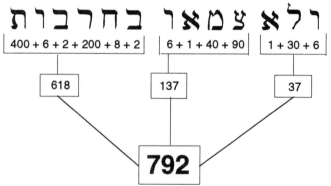

And they thirsted not
in the desert

בחרבות צמאו ולא

| 400 + 6 + 2 + 200 + 8 + 2 | 6 + 1 + 40 + 90 | 1 + 30 + 6 |

| 618 | 137 | 37 |

792

Salvation
ישועות

| 400 + 6 + 70 + 6 + 300 + 10 |

792

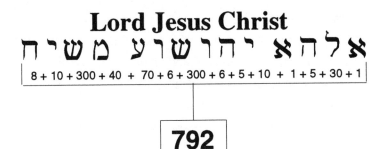

Lord Jesus Christ

אלהא יהושע מ שיח

8 + 10 + 300 + 40 + 70 + 6 + 300 + 6 + 5 + 10 + 1 + 5 + 30 + 1

792

Surely, the blood of Jesus Christ, the means of salvation, was pictured by the water that flowed from the rock. It brought life to the Israelites, and it brings life to all of Adam's race.

In the book of Nehemiah we find again the telling of the story of the rock that gave water. Using the words, exactly as they appear in the Masoretic Text, they read *"water from the rock,"* ומים מסלע, which has a numeric value of 296, (Nehemiah 9:15). Again, it tells the story of salvation through Jesus Christ by its Gematria.

296 = **Water from the rock,** ומים מסלע
2960 = **Son of Man,** υιος του ανθρωπου
296 = **Only begotten,** μονογενη
2960 = **Eternal salvation,** σωτηριας αιωνιου

But, if they indeed carried this rock with them through the desert, why did they, and where did it come from. Surely they had enough to carry through their forty years of wandering without the added weight of a big rock.

Paul told us that *"that Rock was Christ."* In the Greek language, from which Paul's words are translated, the word

"Christ" is the word *"anointed."* Paul was not only suggesting that the rock represented Jesus Christ, but that it was a rock that had been anointed. And indeed we do have the scriptural record of a rock that was anointed, and its Gematria relates to Jesus Christ.

It is the rock that Jacob used as a pillow. Jacob was fleeing from the wrath of his brother Esau, and sought a place of rest for the night. During the night he had a vision in which he saw a ladder reaching from heaven to earth, and angels ascending and descending upon it. And he heard the voice of God confirm to him the covenant that had been given to his grandfather, Abraham, and to his father, Isaac.

Jacob had been profoundly touched! His response came from the utmost depth of his being. He took the stone on which his head had rested, and set it up as a memorial. He anointed it with oil and called it Bethel, which means *"the house of God."* As he poured the oil on the stone, he said, *"And the stone shall become the house of God."*

Jacob was probably not aware of the profound significance of those words. That statement, by its Gematria, points all the way down through time to the One through whom that promised blessing would come – Jesus Christ, that is, Jesus the Anointed. *"And the stone shall become the house of God"* has a numeric value of 592. A square with sides of 592 will have a perimeter of 2368, which is the Gematria for Jesus Christ. It is part of the weaving of the scarlet thread through the history of man.

Whether Jacob took the stone with him at that time, or twenty years later when he returned to that place, the record is not clear. That it was in Jacob's possession is recorded in Genesis 49:24. Jacob, when conferring a blessing on each of his twelve sons, gave a special and significant blessing to Joseph, that he would be strong because of *"The Shepherd, the Stone of Israel."*

The relationship of this stone to the stone which the people of Israel carried with them through the wilderness can be confirmed by its Gematria. They both relate to Jesus Christ.

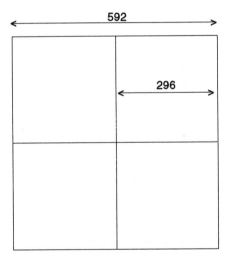

Perimeter 2368

592 = The stone shall become the house of God
296 = Water from the Rock
2368 = Jesus Christ

592 + 296 = 888
888 = Jesus

These numbers have a profound relationship to the circles and squares that have been shown on pages 160 and 161 which show the remarkable relationship of the earth, to the New Jerusalem, Stonehenge, the Great Pyramid and the Molten Sea. This identical pattern now can be seen as it relates to the water from the rock, the Bethel Stone, and the redemptive blood of Jesus Christ, as was poured out on the hill called Golgotha.

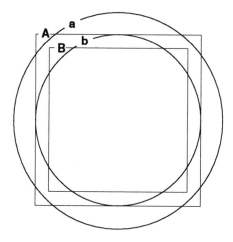

2368 perimeter of square A and circle a
2368 = Jesus Christ

1860 perimeter of square B and circle b
186 = Golgotha

592 one side of Square A and diameter of circle b
592 = And the stone shall become the house of God

296 radius of circle b
296 = water from the rock
2960 = Son of Man

The relationship of these numbers is magnificent! They are telling the story of redemption through the blood of Jesus Christ. They are telling the story of the covenant that was confirmed to Jacob while he laid his head upon the stone. The covenant was that *"all the families of the earth"* would be blessed. The means of that blessing was through the blood of Jesus that was poured out on the hill called Golgotha. That blessing of life was pictured by the water that flowed from the rock.

I was curious to find out a little more about what happened that night to Jacob as he laid his head upon the stone. My research led me to the Book of Jasher. This is a very ancient document that parallels the book of Genesis in the story that it tells. Many Christians do not know of this document. Its antiquity can be affirmed by the fact that the author of the book of Joshua, in the Old Testament, quoted from the Book of Jasher – Joshua 10:13. Even King David quoted from this ancient book during his eulogy of Saul and Jonathan – II Samuel 1:18.

The Book of Jasher tells the story of Jacob fleeing from his brother Esau, and tells of the vision that he had that night, as he slept with his head upon the stone. In Jasher 30:1-3 we find the following information:

> And Jacob went forth continuing his road to Haran, and he came as far as Mount Moriah, and he tarried there all night near the city of Luz; and the Lord appeared there unto Jacob on that night, and he said unto him: I am the Lord God of Abraham and the God of Isaac thy father; the land upon which thou liest I

will give unto thee and thy seed. And behold I am with thee and will keep thee wherever thou goest, and I will multiply thy seed as the stars of Heaven, and I will cause all thine enemies to fall before thee; and when they shall make war with thee they shall not prevail over thee, and I will bring thee again unto this land with joy, with children, and with great riches. And Jacob awoke from his sleep and he rejoiced greatly at the vision which he had seen; and he called the name of that place Bethel.

This account reveals the place where Jacob laid his head that night was on Mount Moriah. In our Bible it only says *"the place"* where he laid his head. Mount Moriah was the hill on which Abraham had offered his son Isaac.

The place where Jacob laid his head was Mount Moriah

Much later, after the city of Jerusalem was built upon that hill, excavations were done which divided the hill. One part is now the Temple mount, and another part of it is the place called Golgotha, where Jesus was crucified. Thus *"the place"* where Jacob laid his head that night – *"the place"* where he received the confirming of the covenant that all the families of the earth would be blessed – was none other than the same hill on which Jesus was crucified. This was the hill where Abraham had offered Isaac. It was the hill where King David had offered sacrifice to God. The hill had become, through time, the meeting place between God and man. It was Golgotha. And this remarkable fact is confirmed by the Gematria.

186 = The place, מקום
186 = Golgotha, Γολγοθα

When Jacob and all his family went down to Egypt at the invitation of Joseph, the stone apparently went with them, for Jacob referred to it when placing his blessing upon Joseph. Having treasured it as a special possession, it would be highly likely that they would have carried it with them on the night they left Egypt. By that time, Moses was their leader. When God instructed Moses to smite the rock, he did not have to ask God "which rock."

The next mention of the rock in the Old Testament account was at the time when Athaliah had assumed the office of king, having killed all the known heirs to the throne. However there was one more heir – a small baby boy. In the seventh year of Athaliah's reign the small seven-year old boy was brought out of hiding and placed upon a pillar in the Temple. The pillar was the cherished stone, which had become the coronation stone. The account reads:

"And when Athaliah heard the noise of the guard and of the people, she came to the people into the temple of the Lord. And when she looked, behold the king stood by (upon) a pillar, as the manner was, and the princes and the trumpeters by the king, and all the people rejoiced, and blew with trumpets. And Athaliah rent her clothes, and cried 'Treason, Treason,'" (II Kings 11:14)

The Hebrew scholar, Isaac Leeser, in his translation of the Old Testament, renders the preposition *"upon"* rather than *"by."* The boy Joash was standing *upon* the pillar.

Leeser goes on to say that this ritual was *"according to custom."*

When Athaliah saw Joash standing on the coronation stone, she knew that he had been proclaimed king. She attempted to flee for her life, but the captains and the officers took her to the horses' stall, and slew her.

Thus we come to know that the nation of Judah had a coronation stone, upon which the kings were officially inducted into office.

Today, the monarchy of England also has a coronation stone, upon which every British monarch who has ruled since James I has been seated for their coronation. Did they copy the idea, or did they indeed have the same stone?

The stone upon which British monarchs receive their coronation came to England from Scotland, and Scottish history tells us that they had obtained it from Ireland. It was the coronation stone upon which the Irish monarchs were crowned. The Irish called it Lea-Fail, which means *"stone of fate,"* or *"stone of destiny."* According to Irish history it had been in their possession, and they had crowned their kings upon it for well over 1,000 years. But where did the Irish kings get their "Lea-Fail?"

The Encyclopedia Britannica (edition 1961) has this to say regarding the Stone of Destiny.

> (Book No. 23, page 540) The coronation chair, which stands in the Confessor's chapel, dates from the time of Edward I and contains beneath its seat the stone of Scone, on which the Scottish kings were crowned. The stone is of Scottish origin, but tradition identifies

it with Jacob's pillow at Bethel.

(Book No. 16, page 790) The inauguration stone of the Irish kings, the Lea-Fail, or Stone of Destiny, fabled to have been the pillow of the patriarch Jacob when he dreamed of the heavenly ladder, was said to have been presented by Murkertagh to the king of Dalriada, by whom it was conveyed to Dunstaffnage castle in Scotland.

(Book No. 12, page 359) Inisfail, a poetic name for Ireland. It is derived from *inis* "island" and Lea-Fail, the celebrated stone identified in Irish legend with the stone on which the patriarch Jacob slept when he dreamed of the heavenly ladder.

Tradition usually has some basis or foundation for its existence. But do we have any evidence in support of this ancient tradition that the stone Lea-Fail was the stone that Jacob used for a pillow?

An analysis of the structure of the stone could determine its origin, if similar rock could be found. Such tests have been made, and to date, no rock formation of its kind has been found in England, Scotland or Ireland. However, on the suggestion of the tradition that this stone came from a place called Bethel, a similar search was made there. It was no surprise to find rock in that vicinity of the same geological structure. A microscopic test of the rock at Bethel matched perfectly with the same test made of the coronation stone. But how did it get from Bethel to Ireland?

Janet and Colin Bord, in their book *Mysterious Britain* (Granada Publishing Limited, London, 1983), have

The Coronation Chair in Westminister Abbey, was built for Edward I in A.D. 1296. The Coronation Stone resides beneath its seat. Every British monarch since Edward I has received their coronation while seated in this chair. The stone resided in England for 1800 years, until it was returned to Scotland in 1996.

capsulized the travels of the stone thus:

> ... no one knows for certain where this stone origi-
> nated nor why it has always had so much significance
> as a stone of inauguration. Traditionally it was the
> pillow used by Jacob when he had his dream of the
> angels at Bethel. Later it was in the Temple of Jerusa-
> lem and the kings of Judah were crowned upon it.
> Then in the fourth century B.C., the daughter of the
> last king of Judah and the prophet Jeremiah travelled
> through Egypt and Spain to Ireland, taking the stone
> with them. The princess from Judah married into the
> royal line of the Irish kings, and for centuries after-
> ward the kings of Ireland were crowned above the
> stone.
>
> Some versions say that it came to Scotland in A.D.
> 500, others say the date was about A.D. 900, but it
> was at a time when the Picts were defeated and one
> of the royal house of Ireland was crowned king of the
> united Scotland. The stone was kept at Scone where
> thirty-four successive Scottish kings were crowned
> sitting above it. In 1297 Edward I took the stone to
> London and had it placed beneath his newly-made
> Coronation Chair in Westminster Abbey. It remained
> there until 1950 when Scottish Nationalists removed
> it and took it into hiding in Scotland. In 1951 it was
> recovered and restored to the Abbey.

In the year 1953, Queen Elizabeth II was crowned,
sitting in the chair, upon the stone.

In the year 1996 the stone, which had resided in

Westminster Abbey, was officially returned to Scotland, accompanied by Prince Andrew, representing the Queen. It was taken to Edinburgh Castle, where it now resides, with the promise that it will be returned, on loan, to London for the coronation of England's next monarch, but will be brought back to Edinburgh Castle for its permanent resting place.

8

The Twins and the Scarlet Thread

Jacob had brought all his family down to Egypt at the invitation of Joseph. After living in Egypt for 17 years, Jacob became ill and knew that he would soon die. He was an old man of 147 years. He gathered his twelve sons to his bedside and conferred a blessing on each of them. It was actually more of a prophecy than a blessing – a prophecy of the *"last days."*

"And Jacob called unto his sons, and said, Gather yourselves together, that I may tell you that which shall befall you in the last days." (Genesis 49:1)

That which he prophesied regarding Judah has profound meaning for the *"last days."*

"Judah, thou art he whom thy brethren shall praise: thy hand shall be in the neck of thine enemies; thy father's children shall bow down before thee. Judah is a lion's whelp: from the prey, my son, thou art gone up: he stooped down, he couched as a lion, and as an old lion; who shall rouse him up? The sceptre shall not depart from Judah, nor a lawgiver from between his feet, until Shiloh come; and unto him shall the gathering of the people be. Binding his foal unto the vine, and his ass's colt unto the choice vine; he washed his garments in wine, and his clothes in the blood of grapes: his eyes shall be red with wine, and his teeth

white with milk." (Genesis 49:8-12)

Instantly we recognize the reference to the scarlet thread. *"He washed his garments in wine, and his clothes in the blood of grapes: his eyes shall be red with wine and his teeth white with milk."* The Hebrew word translated *"red"* means *"sparkling red"* and has a number value of 108. It is a reference to Jesus as the Beginner (1) and the

Red cancels out red, and makes it white.

New Beginner (8). Using this word *"sparkling red"* is another way of saying what Isaiah described: *"Though your sins be as scarlet, they shall be white as snow; though they are red like crimson, they shall be as wool."* In Isaiah's prophecy the words *"they shall be white"* have a numeric value of 108. How remarkable! The red and the white bear the same number – 108.

Again, Isaiah said *"He was pierced"* (Isaiah 53) which also has a numeric value of 108.

The analogy becomes obvious. His red blood, 108 cancels out the red of Adam's sin, 108, and makes us white. The process of making white – *"they shall be white"* – bears the number 108.

When we add red, 108, to red, 108, we obtain 216: (108 + 108 = 216). Jacob's words *"He shall wash his clothes in the blood of grapes"* describes the transaction. *"The blood of grapes"* adds to 216. The numbers are not random. They are obviously an integral part of the story of the scarlet thread.

The words that Jacob prophesied regarding Judah tell of rulership. He said that Judah's brothers would bow down to him. He said the sceptre would not depart from Judah until the coming of Shiloh. The symbol of the sceptre means having the right to rule. Thus we would expect that Judah's descendants would become kings. And surely they did.

The first king to come from the line of Judah was King David. His kingdom was a type of the reign of King Messiah – the Lion of the Tribe of Judah – who is of the lineage of Judah through David. When He comes as Shiloh He takes His rightful place as ruler on the throne of

Shiloh will take His rightful place as ruler.

David. Amazingly, this prophecy gives us a time-line for that rulership, by its Gematria. It was skillfully and magnificently encoded into the text with the use of the Golden Proportion – the Divine Proportion. It not only tells of the 1,000 years from the time when David was anointed king over all Israel, and set up his seat of government in Jerusalem, to the birth of the One born to be the rightful king, Jesus, but it also tells of the 3,000 years from King David to King Messiah (Shiloh). And as an added feature, it tells us of the 4,000 years from King David to the full completion of the Millennial Kingdom and the beginning of the Great Eighth Day – God's Grand Octave of time.

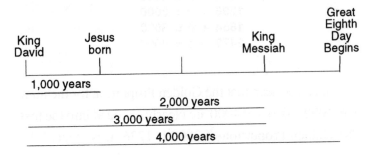

Below is the Hebrew Masoretic text for this prophecy. Remember, Hebrew reads from right to left, and thus when showing the word-for-word translation, the English must also be read from right to left.

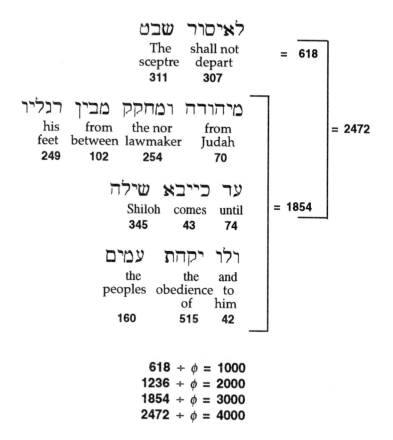

לא׳סור שבט

The sceptre	shall not depart
311	307

= 618

מיהורה ומחקק מבין רגליו

his feet	from between	the nor lawmaker	from Judah
249	102	254	70

= 2472

עד כייבא שילה

Shiloh	comes	until
345	43	74

= 1854

ולו יקהת עמים

the peoples	the obedience of	and to him
160	515	42

$$618 \div \phi = 1000$$
$$1236 \div \phi = 2000$$
$$1854 \div \phi = 3000$$
$$2472 \div \phi = 4000$$

It can be seen that the Golden Proportion for the numbers 1000, 3000 and 4000 are clearly encoded into the text. The Golden Proportion of 2000 is 1236. It is evident that this number is part of the pattern, for when Isaiah foretold the time of Jesus's birth, he said, *"Therefore the Lord Himself shall give you a sign, Behold, a virgin shall be with child and shall bring forth a son; and she shall call His name Immanuel."* Matthew quoted this in relating the events of Jesus' birth. He said the name Immanuel means *"God with us,"* μεθ ημων Θεος. It has a number value of 1236. It is the Golden Proportion of 2000 and relates to the 2,000 years from the birth of Jesus to the time when King Messiah becomes the rightful Ruler.

Judah was promised rulership. But that rulership would only go to his descendants. In the course of time, Judah's daughter-in-law, Tamar, was pregnant by Judah. He had mistaken her for a harlot, and had gone in unto her. When it came time for her to be delivered, it was found that she had twins in her womb.

"And it came to pass, when she travailed, that the one put out his hand; and the midwife took and bound upon his hand a scarlet thread, saying, This came out first. And it came to pass, as he drew back his hand, that, behold, his brother came out: and she said, How hast thou broken forth? this breach be upon thee: therefore his name was called Pharez. And afterward came out his brother, that had the scarlet thread upon his hand: and his name was called Zerah." (Genesis 38:28-30)

It is more than just a story in ancient history. The midwife tied a scarlet thread around the hand that came out first, probably thinking that this child would continue to be the firstborn, and in the excitement and haste of the birth of two babies, instead of one, she wanted to make sure she identified which one was truly the firstborn. But it did not work that way. This child drew his hand back in, and the other twin was born first. The midwife had no way of knowing that this would happen. She was merely trying to identify the firstborn.

So – which baby was the firstborn? Was it Zerah, with the scarlet thread tied around his hand; or was it Pharez who came out first? Or, do you suppose the story happened the way it did because *both* babies were Tamar's firstborn. They were twins, thus they both were the firstborn. I began to realize this when I saw the Gematria of their names. Each child has interesting Gematria for his name, but the combination of both names tells the story. Both Zerah and Pharez have Gematria that relates to the blood of Jesus and His position as the rightful Ruler who will sit on David's throne. And the addition of both their names produces numbers that relate to the time when He comes with His bride to set up His kingdom. The numbers are truly amazing!

Zerah
זרח
8 + 200 + 7

215

The Blood of Jesus
τω αιματι Ιησου

| 300 + 800 + 1 + 10 + 40 + 1 + 300 + 10 + 10 + 8 + 200 + 70 + 400 |

2150

tied on his hand scarlet
שני   על-ידו   תקשר

| 10 + 50 + 300 + 6 + 4 + 10 + 30 + 70 + 200 + 300 + 100 + 400 |

1480

B l o o d
נ צ ח

| 8 + 90 + 50 |

148

Christ
Χριστος

| 600+100+10+200+300+70+200 |

1480

Can we deny that the name Zerah and the tying of the scarlet thread around his hand represents the blood of Jesus Christ? The Gematria is simple and obvious, and there for all to see. They are not random numbers. They are numbers with purpose and meaning.

The same applies to the name Pharez. He was given this name because the midwife was upset with the fact that he came out before the baby with the scarlet thread. She scolded him and asked why did he have the right to break forth before his brother. So she called him "The Breaker" or "The Breach." The Gematria of his name reveals that he truly will be a Ruler, and from his line will come the Messiah.

Pharez

פ ר ץ

90 + 200 + 80

370

Ruler

מ ש ל

30 + 300 + 40

370

My Messiah

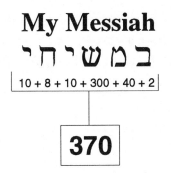

ב מ ש י ח י

10 + 8 + 10 + 300 + 40 + 2

370

The number 37 is the 12th prime, and its multiples are the names and titles of Jesus. In Psalm 105:15 God is speaking of *"My Messiah"* or *"My Anointed"* – for the Hebrew word messiah means anointed. It reminds us of the rock they carried with them in the wilderness. It had been anointed by Jacob; and the Apostle Paul said that Rock was Christ. Christ is the Greek word for anointed. In chapter one we saw the Gematria for the waters that flowed from the rock was 1480.

1480 = Christ
1480 = He opened the rock and the
           waters gushed out; they ran in
           the dry places

Zerah bears the number 215, and Pharez bears the number 370. But we are considering the two as one – both representing Jesus Christ whose shed blood is the scarlet thread of redemption; and who also represent the One coming to save Israel from her enemies and set up His Kingdom of Peace in the earth.

Since we are considering the twins as one, let's add the numbers of their names. What a surprise was in store for me when I did this. I was grasping for understanding because I could not discern the meaning.

Zerah	215
Pharez	370
	585

585 = A pillar of stone, מצבת אבן
(The anointed stone, Genesis 35:14)

585 = That Just One, τον δικαιον
(Referring to Jesus, Acts 22:14)

585 = The Lord my God shall come and all the saints,
ובא יהוה אלהי כל-קרשים
(Speaking of the time when He comes with His bride to put an end to Armageddon and set up His Kingdom in the earth, Zechariah 14:5)

Addition is not the only function of Gematria. When multiplying the number values of the names of the twins, we find they also point to Jesus in a most beautiful way. Surely we have evidence that both twins represent Jesus and the work of salvation and restoration. One had the scarlet thread on his hand, and the other came out first, but together they represent the fulfilling of the work of redemption, the setting up of the Kingdom of peace, and the restoring to man of all that had been lost through the sin of Adam.

The Apostle Peter wrote concerning this work of redemption by Christ Jesus, and the titles that he used for Jesus refer all the way back to Zerah and Pharez by their Gematria. He said:

"... Who his own self bare our sins in his own body on the tree.... For ye were as sheep going astray; but are now returned unto the Shepherd and Bishop of your souls. (I Peter 2:24-25)

The multiplication of the number equivalents for the names of Zerah and Pharez, when combined, produce the number 256. The addition of the number equivalents, when combined, produce the number 585. The titles that Peter used are precisely these two numbers.

	by addition	by multiplication
Zerah	**215**	**112**
Pharez	**370**	**144**
	585	**256**

Shepherd, ποιμενα = **256**
Bishop, επισκοπον = **585**

The evidence appears to tell us that both Zerah and Pharez, as one unit, represent the work of redemption and restoration through Jesus Christ. One carried the scarlet thread upon his hand, and the other broke forth first.

The name Zerah means *"Rising of light,"* Isaiah used this Hebrew word when prophesying of the time when Jesus would come and bring *"light"* to Israel; and through Israel to all the Gentiles. He said:

The name Zerah means "the rising of light."

"Arise, shine; for thy light is come, and the glory of the Lord is risen upon thee. For, behold, the darkness shall cover the earth, and gross darkness the people: but the Lord shall arise upon thee, and his glory shall be seen upon thee. And the Gentiles shall come to thy light, and kings to the brightness of thy rising." (Isaiah 60:1-3)

Isaiah was prophesying of the time when Jesus will sit on the throne of David. Further in this same chapter, Isaiah went on to say:

"The sons also of them that afflicted thee shall come bending unto thee; and all they that despised thee shall bow themselves down at the soles of thy feet; and they shall call the, The City of the Lord, The Zion of the Holy One of Israel." (verse 14)

That is the meaning of the name Zerah. When Jesus said, *"I am the light of the world"* He was fulfilling that which was typified by the name Zerah.

256 = Zerah & Pharez (by multiplication)
256 = To give light, נור, (by addition)

The name Pharez means *"to break forth,"* or *"to breach."* The prophet Micah used this word as a title for the One who would deliver Israel from their enemies. He called him *"the Breaker"* and he also called him *"their King." "The Breaker is come up before them: they have broken up, and have passed through the gate, and are gone out by it: and their king shall pass before them, and the Lord on the head of them."* (Micah 2:13)

The name Pharez means "The Breaker."

His role as The Breaker is described in Revelation 19:11-16, when He comes to put an end to Armageddon and to save His people Israel from destruction.

"And I saw heaven opened, and behold a white horse; and he that sat upon him was called Faithful and True, and in righteousness he doth judge and make war. His eyes were as a flame of fire, and on his head were many crowns; and he had a name written, that no man knew, but he himself. And he was clothed with a vesture dipped in blood; and his name is called The Word of God. And the armies which were in heaven followed him upon white horses, clothed in fine linen, white and clean. And out of his mouth goeth a sharp sword, that with it he should smite the nations; and he shall rule them with a rod of iron: and he treadeth the winepress of the fierceness and wrath of Almighty God. And he hath on his vesture and on his thigh a name written, KING OF KINGS, AND LORD OF LORDS."

Among the constellations – the *"signs in the heavens"* – is one called *"The Breaker."* His other name is Perseus. He is shown as a warrior, holding high a sword in his right hand, and securely tucked under his left arm is the severed head of the enemy. The bright star in this severed head is called *Al Gol,* or in Hebrew it is called *Rosh Satan* – the head of the adversary.

The reason this starry figure is called Perseus is because it is taken from the Hebrew word *"Pharez"* which means *"The Breaker."* The name is used prophetically of Jesus in Isaiah 58:12: *"and you shall be called the Repairer of the Breach, the Restorer of paths to live in."*

In recent years something very remarkable happened in the constellation Perseus, involving the severed head that he holds under his left arm. It possibly is a sign to those who are watching for the fulfillment of prophecy regarding the end time.

On the night of April 11, 1996, the comet Hyakutake was positioned precisely over the star *Al Gol,* the bright star in the severed head of Satan. Then, precisely one solar year later, on the night of April 11, 1997, the comet Hale-Bopp was also positioned precisely over *Al Gol.* The paths of these two comets came at right angles to each other, forming a cross on the forehead of the head of Satan, which Perseus holds under his left arm. That the paths of these two comets crossed at right angles precisely over *Al Gol,* and precisely one year apart, is astounding! Was it a sign?

We are told in the Bible that the stars were to be for signs. And we are also told that there would be signs in the heavens regarding the time of Jesus' return. It is exciting to realize that April 11, 1996 and April 11, 1997, which joined the paths of these two comets, forming a cross, was followed by the occurrence of Passover on April 11, 1998.

The years 1996 and 1997 formed the image of the cross, and that same date in 1998 was the anniversary of the day when Jesus hung on that cross, and died – the fulfillment of the promise of the scarlet thread. The chances against this having been sheer coincidence are astronomical!

Perseus – The Breaker

Micah had prophesied *"The Breaker has come up."* That statement has a numeric value of 480. It is a number that is associated with the coming of Jesus in the *"last days."* Jesus spoke of this same event, and stated it in plain terms. He called it, *"The coming of the Son of Man."* (Matthew 24:27) Both statements bear the same number. It is a number that is associated with the time of Jesus' return.

480 = The Breaker has come up
4800 = The coming of the Son of Man

In Psalm 106 we find another prophetic statement regarding the work of The Breaker – He is the One who stands in the breach.

888 = "His chosen one stood before him in the breach"
888 = Jesus

In the Psalm, this is spoken of Moses when he pleaded with God to save Israel, but it is prophetic of Jesus when He comes to save Israel from destruction.

The first coming of Jesus was for the purpose of sacrifice – to shed His innocent blood to pay the price for the sin of Adam. The second coming of Jesus is for the purpose of claiming His rightful place as King on David's throne. This two-fold work was typified by Melchisedec, who was both a priest and a king. The writer of the book of Hebrews gave a lengthy explanation of this dual office which Jesus holds. I will quote portions of it, trying to touch the key concepts.

"... it is evident that our Lord sprang out of Judah; of which tribe Moses spake nothing concerning priesthood. And it is yet far more evident: for that after the similitude of Melchisedec there ariseth another priest ... For he testifieth, Thou art a priest forever after the order of Melchisedec." (Hebrews 7)

In this 7th chapter of Hebrews, the analogy is being made between Melchisedec, who was both a priest and a king, and Jesus, who also is both Priest and King.

The function of a priest is to offer sacrifice. This Jesus did when He offered His body and His **Zerah pictures the priesthood of Jesus.** blood upon Calvary's cross. He offered himself.

The function of a king is to rule with power and authority. This Jesus does when He comes the second time, to take His rightful place on the throne of David, and set up His kingdom of peace. Melchisedec was called *"King of Peace."*

This dual function of Priest and King was typified by Judah's twin boys. Zerah put forth his arm, and the mid-wife tied a scarlet thread on his hand. But Pharez actually came out first. Zerah, the child with the **Pharez pictures the kingship of Jesus.** scarlet thread, pictures the office of Priest, making sacri-fice and the shedding of blood. Pharez, from whose line came King David, is a type of the kingship of Jesus, when He comes as the rightful Ruler on David's throne.

These twin boys pictured the work of the first coming (sacrifice) of Jesus, and the second coming (reigning) of

Jesus. The one who wore the scarlet thread pictured sacrifice and the shedding of blood. The one who came out first pictured rulership and authority.

This dual function as both Priest and King was beautifully pictured by Judah's twin boys. In the typology of the Bible, they both pictured Jesus, therefore one did not have the position of "firstborn" over the other. And again, the Gematria confirms the meaning. These are not random numbers. They are numbers with a purpose!

215 = **Zerah** (by addition)
2150 = **The Blood of Jesus,** $\tau\omega \; \alpha\iota\mu\alpha\tau\iota \; I\eta\sigma\sigma\upsilon$

112 = **Zerah** (by multiplication)
112 = **High Priest,** גרל כהן

370 = **Pharez** (by addition)
370 = **To reign,** משל
37 = **Power,** אול
370 = **He shall rule wisely,** ישכיל, (Isaiah 52:13)

144 = **Pharez** (by multiplication)
144 = **David their King,** דוד מלכם (prophetic of Jesus), (Jeremiah 30:9)
144 = **Lord Christ,** $K\upsilon\rho\iota\sigma\nu \; X\rho\iota\sigma\tau\sigma\nu$, (Acts 2:36)

9

Tying It All Together

The story of the scarlet thread has taken us on a journey through time. It reveals a plan, a purpose, a destination and an outcome. And it tells a consistent story – the story of the fall, judgment, redemption, restitution, and restoration of man.

Even before Adam was created, the plan was set in motion. The redemptive blood was already promised.

Adam was created perfect, and placed into a perfect condition in the Garden of Eden. He was given a perfect law. He chose to disobey that law, and hence brought upon himself the penalty for disobedience – death. All of his posterity inherited that death penalty.

But God did not leave Adam and his race in that hopeless condition. Throughout the pages of time God has given to man the picture of what He purposed to do for man's salvation. It was the picture of the scarlet thread. That thread has been woven into the entire history of man. Yes, man's history is tied together with a scarlet thread.

Innocent blood was first shed for man so that he could be clothed. Again, innocent blood was shed by Abel as he offered to God the sacrifice of one from his flock. The innocent blood of Isaac was accounted as offered on the altar on Mount Moriah. But God provided a ram who stood in Isaac's place. The innocent blood of a lamb was painted on the doorframes of the homes of the Israelites on that last night they were in Egypt. All who were in the house were *"under the blood"* and escaped death. When they left Egypt, under the leadership of Moses, they carried with them a stone from which they obtained water. That water represented life through the shed blood of Jesus.

That stone, from which they obtained water, was first given to Jacob on Mount Moriah, where he anointed it and named it Bethel – the House of God.

On the afternoon of April 3, A.D. 33, Jesus hung on a cross on Mount Moriah (by this time called Calvary and Golgotha). His innocent blood was poured out upon the ground. It was there that He gave His life for the life of Adam. His innocent blood was the scarlet thread that has tied all history together into one common purpose – the redemption and restoration of man.

The story of the life-giving blood of Jesus Christ is also told by the Golden Proportion, which has come to be known as the Divine Proportion. We have seen that the place where that redemptive blood was shed defines a Golden Proportion.

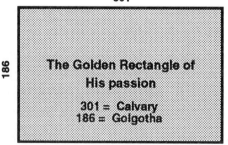

When the midwife tied the scarlet thread on the hand of Zerah, little did she know that this child would represent the greatest event in the history of man – the shedding of the redemptive blood for the sin of Adam. But God led her to tie the scarlet thread around the baby's hand. When Moses recorded this unusual birth, little did he know that the number values of the letters would tell the story of redemption. No, but it was encoded into the text by the hand of God, and has come down to us in all its beauty.

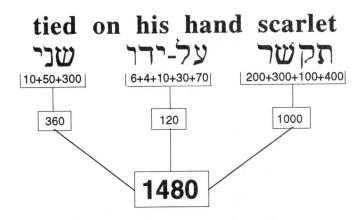

A square having sides of 370 will have a perimeter of 1480. We have seen that the number 37 is a prime that always relates to the work of redemption through Jesus Christ. If we project the Golden Proportion of this square, we find the key figure in the whole work of redemption – Jesus. His number is eloquently displayed there by the Golden Spiral that can be inscribed within the rectangle. These three numbers, 1480, 370 and 888 tie together the story of the scarlet thread.

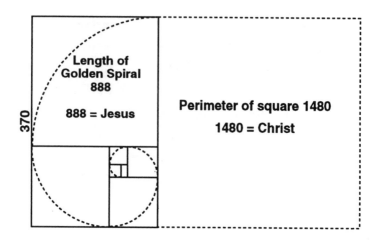

1480 = Tied on his hand scarlet

1480 = He opened the rock and the
waters gushed out; they ran in the
dry places.

1480 = Blood

148 = Passover (the killing of the lamb)

1480 = Christ (He was the Lamb)

148 = Scales (the balancing of justice)

148 = Victory

1480 = Son of God

1480 = His Kingdom

370 = My Messiah (the Anointed One)

370 = He reigns

370 = The Breaker (He comes to break
through Israel's enemies, and set up
His Kingdom.)

888 = Jesus
888 = I am the Life
888 = Salvation of our God

When Simeon held the baby Jesus in his arms, he praised God and exclaimed, *"Now my eyes have seen thy salvation."* He had seen the *"salvation of God."* He held in his arms the baby whose name was 888, and he knew it was the promised Messiah.

He came the first time to offer His life as a sacrifice – to shed His innocent blood for the sin of Adam. He comes the second time to take His rightful place as King on the Throne of David. Today we stand on the threshold of that promised Kingdom. And, just as surely as He came the first time, in fulfillment of all the promises and types and pictures; just as assuredly He comes the second time to set up His Kingdom.

His Kingdom

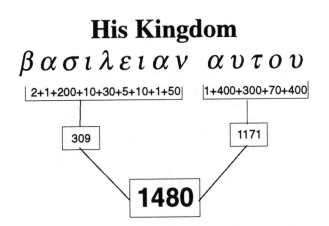

The Apostle Paul tied it all together in a few short verses in I Corinthians 15. He described the entire 7,000 years, followed by the great Eighth Day in which man is again in the perfection which was originally given to him.

"For as in Adam all die, even so in Christ shall all be made alive. But every man in his own order: Christ the firstfruits; afterward they that are Christ's at his coming.

"Then cometh the end, when he shall have delivered up the kingdom to God, even the Father; when he shall have put down all rule and all authority and power. For he must reign till he hath put all enemies under his feet. The last enemy that shall be destroyed is death.

"For he hath put all things under his feet.... And when all things shall be subdued unto him, then shall the Son also himself be subject unto him that put all things under him, that God may be all in all." (verses 22-28)

Jesus is the Beginner, symbolized by the number 1, and the New Beginner, symbolized by the number 8. His work as the New Beginner is shown in Paul's words by their Gematria:

8888 = He must reign till he hath put all enemies under his feet.

His role as the Beginner and the New Beginner are shown by His Revelation to John, for He said, *"I am the Alpha and the Omega, the first and the last."* (Rev. 1:11) He was saying "I am the One and the Eight" for Alpha is the first letter of the Greek alphabet, equivalent to the number 1; and Omega is the last letter of the Greek alphabet, equivalent to the number 800.

Both 1 and 8 define scarlet.

108 = Red, חכלילי
800 = Vermillion,ששר
108 x 8 = 864

Daniel saw this Kingdom that would be given to Jesus, and the Gematria of the words he recorded reveal the importance of the 1 and the 8.

"I saw in the night visions, and, behold one like the Son of man came with clouds of heaven, and came to the Ancient of days, and they brought him near before him. And there was given him dominion, and glory, and a kingdom, that all people, nations, and languages, should serve him: his dominion is an everlasting dominion, which shall not pass away, and his kingdom that which shall not be destroyed." (Daniel 7:13-14)

864 = There was given him dominion, and glory, and a kingdom

He was the Lamb slain from the foundation of the world. It is His redemptive blood which restores all that Adam lost, providing Adam and his race a New Beginning. This is the story of the scarlet thread, weaving its way through the history of man. God knew from the beginning that man would sin and would need a Redeemer. And the entrance of sin did not thwart His original intention that man should live in perfection in the beautiful home that He had made for him – planet earth.

This is why scarlet bears the number 360. It describes a circle – the great circle of time – 7,000 years from man's fall to his complete restoration. This is why "the scarlet" bears the number 365. It describes the circle of time in which earth moves around its source of light and life. Yes, the whole plan of God for the life of man upon this earth is tied together with a scarlet thread.

Appendix I
Gematria: how it works

All creation, from the largest to the smallest, can always be reduced to numbers. Pythagoras, the father of mathematics, discovered a great truth when he said "Numbers are the language of the universe." In the writings of the ancient philosophers there is common agreement that the purpose of number is for the investigation of the universe. From the atom to the galaxy in the heavens, the same unchanging laws apply – the laws of arithmetic, the language of number.

Just as the hand of God spread the vast expanse of the heavens by number, so too His written word can be reduced to number; and those who have tried it have stood in awe of the intricacy and beauty of the design. It was an intentional design.

The secrets locked up in the Number Code of the Bible are there for all to behold; and down through the centuries many have unlocked those secrets and revealed to us the unspeakable beauty of the intended design. Part of the numerical design of the scriptures is the science of Gematria.

The Old Testament was originally written in the Hebrew language, and the New Testament in Greek. These two languages used the letters of their alphabets for symbols of amount. Their alphabets were called "dual character systems" – one of sound, or phonetics, and the other of amount, or number.

Tobias Dantzig, a professor of mathematics at the University of Maryland (U.S.A.) explained the phenomenon thus:[1]

> The sum of the numbers represented by the letters of the word was the number of the word, and from the standpoint of Gematria two words were equivalent if they added up to the same number. Not only was Gematria used from the earliest days for the interpretation of Biblical passages, but there are indications that the writers of the Bible had practiced the art. Thus Abraham proceeding to rescue his brother Eliasar drives forth 318 slaves. Is it just a coincidence that the Hebrew word Eliasar adds up to 318?

Within the first century A.D., Barnabas, the traveling companion of the Apostle Paul, wrote concerning this number code.

> For the scripture says that Abraham circumcised three hundred and eighteen men of his house. But what therefore was the mystery that was made known unto him? Mark, first the eighteen, and next the three hundred. For the numeral letters of ten and eight are I H. And these denote Jesus. And because the cross was that by which we were to find grace; therefore he adds three hundred; the note of which is T (the figure of his cross). Wherefore by two letters he signified Jesus, and by the third his cross.

Barnabas leads us to realize that the knowledge of the

---

1 Tobias Dantzig, *Number, the Language of Science,* Doubleday Anchor Books, New York, NY, 1930, p. 40.

use of Gematria in the word of God is not something of modern discovery.

One of the best known demonstrations of Gematria in the Old Testament is the section headings in Psalm 119. Any student of the Old Testament is aware that the names for these sections are in fact the sequential letters of the Hebrew alphabet. These letters were simply used to number the sections. In some Bibles the word for the letter is spelled out, (such as *aleph*); while in other translations, the single letter is used (such as א) – both of these translate, by Gematria, to the number 1.

Gematria among the Greeks was in common use at the time of the writing of the New Testament. A copy of one of these early manuscripts, called *papyri*, (because they were written on papyrus) exists today in Dublin, Ireland in the Chester Beatty Collection. It is the earliest known copy of the book of Revelation extant. It is dated somewhere between 200 and 300 A.D. This manuscript uses Gematria for every number in the book of Revelation.

The re-discovery of these Number Codes is not new. The noted Bible expositor, E. W. Bullinger, was among the many who have added to our understanding of this subject. His book *Number in Scripture,* published in 1894, shows the supernatural design in the use of numbers, both in the works of God and in the word of God.

The number equivalents for the Greek alphabet can be found in any Webster's Dictionary.

The Greek alphabet used twenty six letters, two of which have become extinct. The current twenty four are listed below:

Alpha	α	1
Beta	β	2
Gamma	γ	3
Delta	δ	4
Epsilon	ε	5
Zeta	ζ	7
Eta	η	8
Theta	θ	9
Iota	ι	10
Kappa	κ	20
Lambda	λ	30
Mu	μ	40
Nu	ν	50
Xi	ξ	60
Omicron	o	70
Pi	π	80
Rho	ρ	100
Sigma	$\sigma \varsigma$	200
Tau	τ	300
Upsilon	υ	400
Phi	ϕ	500
Chi	χ	600
Psi	ψ	700
Omega	ω	800

There were once letters for 6 and 90, but they became obsolete through time, and finally dropped from the alphabet. The letter standing for the number 6 was called "stigma." It looked similar to sigma. The only use for the letter stigma in the New Testament is in Revelation 13:18 where it gives the number of the one who comes as the imposter of Christ. In the old manuscripts it was written as $\chi\xi\varsigma = 600, 60, 6$. Thus when added they become 666.

The Hebrew alphabet is, in many ways, quite similar to the Greek. However, rather than 24 letters, it uses only 22 letters.

Aleph	א	1
Beth	ב	2
Gimel	ג	3
Daleth	ד	4
He	ה	5
Vav	ו	6
Zayin	ז	7
Cheth	ח ך	8
Teth	ט	9
Yod	י	10
Kaph	כ	20
Lamed	ל	30
Mem	ם מ	40
Nun	ן נ	50
Camek	ס	60
Ayin	ע	70
Pe	ף פ ך	80
Tsadey	ץ צ	90
Qoph	ק	100
Resh	ר	200
Shin	ש	300
Tav	ת	400

Notice there are five finals. These letters are shaped differently when they appear as the final letter in a word. In the Cabala these five finals are given higher numbers, namely, 500, 600, 700, 800 and 900. In my search of the Gematria of the Bible, I do not find this additional assigning of the numbers to be part of the original design. It was an addition to the system, which was adopted later.

It should be noted that according to the rules of Gematria, one unit called *colel* could be added or subtracted from a word or phrase without changing its meaning. I have avoided the use of *colel* in this book.

Books by Bonnie Gaunt

THE BIBLE'S AWESOME NUMBER CODE
$14.95

THE COMING OF JESUS
The Real Message of the Bible Codes!
$14.95

JESUS CHRIST
The Number of His Name
$12.95

BEGINNINGS
The Sacred Design
$14.95

STONEHENGE AND THE GREAT PYRAMID
Window on the Universe
$12.95

THE STONES CRY OUT
God's Best Kept Secrets Hidden in Stone
$9.95

THE MAGNIFICENT NUMBERS
of the Great Pyramid and Stonehenge
$9.95

STONEHENGE
A Closer Look
$9.95

All of the above books explore the exciting science of
Gematria, the Number Code of the Bible.